What People are Saying About
Gotta Get 'em Fixed!

"Through my speaking, teaching, and writing, I hope to point people to the Lord. That is why I am so excited about this book and Twila's clear and creative approach to seeing life through God's eyes. It is a great resource."
—Marita Littauer, President of CLASServices, Inc., speaker and author of *You've Got What It Takes* and *Love Extravagantly*

"Twila's fresh, humorous approach to driving home biblical truth will leave a smile on your face and a lasting impression on your heart."
—Florence Littauer, President of CLASS Speakers, Inc. and author of 30 books on personal growth, including *Personality Plus* and *Silver Boxes*

"Using wit and wisdom, Twila gives us a wonderful glimpse of life and of God! With her light-hearted approach, she encourages us to keep our eyes fixed on the Lord."
—Georgia Shaffer, Christian Life Coach and author of *A Gift of Mourning Glories*

"Read this book! Not just because it's hilariously funny, insightful, and packed with spiritual truth, but because I'm Twila's husband and I said so!"
—Steve Belk, Twila's husband and a great resource for writing material

SPIRITUAL OPHTHALMOLOGY 101

Gotta Get 'em Fixed!

SPIRITUAL OPHTHALMOLOGY 101

God bless you!
Twila Belk
Prov. 3:5,6
☺

Twila Belk

WINEPRESS WP PUBLISHING

Packaged by WinePress Publishing, PO Box 428, Enumclaw, WA 98022. The views expressed or implied in this work do not necessarily reflect those of WinePress Publishing. The author(s) is ultimately responsible for the design, content, and editorial accuracy of this work.

ISBN 1-57921-429-0
Library of Congress Catalog Card Number: 2001097751

To the only wise God be glory forever
through Jesus Christ!

Foreword

I don't know that I am writing a foreword to a book as much as I'm introducing you to a person, because this book *is* Twila Belk. Her wit, her personality, her years of walking with the Lord—it all spills out here, all over the pages, as she shares. As I think of Twila, sportscaster Dick Enberg's favorite phrase comes to mind: "Oh, my!"

I first met Twila and husband Steve in StraightWay, the Christian bookstore they ran for nine years. I wasn't a very regular customer, since I lived and ministered on the other side of the Mississippi River. But occasionally I'd cross the border and venture into the store in search of something new or different. It didn't take long to learn what kind of folks these were—with Twila nothing is held back. (Those who know her are no doubt laughing at this understatement!) StraightWay was a great place to just "hang" for a while; you always felt at home there.

I didn't know them well when tragedy struck, but well enough that I hurt inside on hearing the news of the auto accident. It was one more way God was at work preparing

the heart of a future author. As you read these pages, you'll
see that while fun and laughter appear to dominate her life,
Twila has been through deep waters as well. She has a vast
array of life experiences to draw upon and a keen sense of
what God is teaching her through each one. With her unique
way of drawing you right inside those experiences, I'm con-
fident you'll learn from them, too.

For the past seven years, I have served as pastor to Steve
and Twila, and now it's my privilege to turn her loose on
you. This past spring I did a sermon series on the "one
another" commands in the New Testament, integrating first-
hand testimony whenever I could. When I came to the
phrase "speak to one another," there was no question who
I'd share the pulpit with that morning. Twila loves to speak
. . . and speak . . . and speak—because she's just "gotta tell
somebody!"

I've lived through many of the incidents set forth in the
book, from the Skunk Sighting to The Big Announcement.
How could we ever forget that one? Seems I addressed Steve
as "Abraham" from the pulpit that day. The memories come
pouring back vividly as I read. But believe me, they'll be
plenty vivid for you, too. Twila has a unique, down-to-earth
style (understatement #2!) that just sort of plops you right
down next to her as she tells it. It's about slices of real life,
things we can all relate to, lessons we can all benefit from.
So, sit back and enjoy the ride! I know I did.

Rick Smith
Senior Pastor
Pleasant View Baptist Church
Bettendorf, Iowa

Introduction

Eat more carrots! If only the answer were so easy. Our family sat around the supper table crunching carrots when daughter Laney claimed that downing more of this vegetable would result in better eyesight. I remember my mom telling me the same thing years ago. As a child and even as an adult I diligently consumed my fair share of carrots, and I always proudly proclaimed my great vision.

Apparently, Bugs Bunny lives by this philosophy as well. He eats carrots continuously and hasn't worn glasses a day in his life. I'm sure the carrot industry benefits tremendously from such a popular endorsement of their product. But, I'm going to let you in on a little secret. I hope you won't be overly disappointed. Bugs Bunny is just a cartoon character. Do you know what that means? Bugs Bunny will never experience a 40th birthday! Bugs Bunny will never learn that all the carrots in the world can't help the one who's crossed the line from 39.

Sadly to say I've learned, though. So has my husband. There's something mysterious and magical that happens in your sleep the night you hit 40. I don't know how this process works, but you wake up to find your arms are no longer long enough. You can't read without enlisting a helper to hold your papers a couple feet away. Numbers begin blurring together. A 5 looks like a 6 and a 6 like an 8. Once familiar letters in the alphabet become like blended blobs. You can't tell your children apart until you hear them speak. Oh, the joys of aging! (On an encouraging note, I must admit I appreciate having an excuse that works for everything. When I can't see or hear right, or if I do something air-headed, I simply state that I'm over 40. People immediately understand.)

Lately Steve and I have been getting more and more frustrated with our eyesight. It seems we strain harder every day to see clearly. Therefore, we've decided that it's time. We gotta get our eyes fixed! Now if one of us could only read the numbers in the phone book, we could maybe call the eye doctor for an appointment!

I've noticed other things come into our lives that muddle up our vision, too. And age makes no difference at all. The things are many—skunks, giants, weather, worry, pity, tight spots, bad days, fleabites, rude intruders, stinkin' thinkin', pride. The list goes on and on. Sometimes our vision becomes so clouded over or hazy that we can't focus on anything but self or circumstances. Once again, carrots won't help. The solution is simple, though. We gotta get our eyes fixed on Almighty God and on His Word.

The benefits of getting our eyes fixed are many. We learn how big God is and how much He loves us. We start to trust more and worry less. We see God at work in every detail and every situation, good or bad. We find that all of a sudden everything looks a whole lot better. When our focus is on God, we start to view life from His perspective. This affects our attitudes, our actions, our choices, the way we handle the tough stuff that comes our way, and the way we respond to Him.

Gotta Get 'em Fixed! is a result of what God has been teaching me through His course in Spiritual Ophthalmology. It's an ongoing course, and I learn something new everyday, but I've noticed the quizzes and exams become easier and easier with time. Getting and keeping my eyes fixed has gradually become more of a lifestyle and less of a struggle. But I have to be careful. The things that cause vision problems continuously lurk close by, just waiting to give me a good case of eyestrain. I have to make a deliberate choice daily to focus on God.

As you read the following pages I hope you'll "bust a gut" laughing with me, and I hope the smile on your face will seep to your heart and stay there. Most importantly, though, I pray you'll discover as I have that you can't lose when your eyes are fixed on our wonderful Lord.

Contents

Skunk Sighting 19

In a Fix 23

Big Honkin' Words 29

Reproducing 35

Tight Spots 39

The StraightWay Experience 43

Fresh Dirt 51

Bad Days 55

Whatever, Lord! 59

Ponderings 65

Now, That's Embarrassing! 69

Mitad Del Mundo 73

A New Heart 79

The Big Announcement 85

The Rude Intruders 89

Mud Bath 97

Orphaned 103

Surprise! 109

Weirdin' Out 115

Lessons from a Sixteen-Month-Old 119

I Yam What I Yam 125

Gotta Tell Somebody! 131

Ointments 139

An Interview with the Virtuous Woman 143

Trash or Treasure? 149

Potato Words 155

Toenail Love 159

Born to Sell 163

A New Wardrobe 167

No Comprendo 173

It Shows 177

The Fishin' Foot 183

Garbage Can Freedom 187

Choices 193

Contents

Getting Married 197

Driving Home a Point 205

The Rest of the Story 209

Choose Your Own Ending 219

    #1 – I Did It My Way 220

    #2 – Sittin' on the Fence 224

    #3 – Sold Out and Having the Ride of My Life 230

Skunk Sighting

We had a predicament on our hands. I'm talking bad—really bad. A black-and-white predicament.

Our two-car garage is attached to a smaller, shed-type garage with a dirt floor. This shed-type garage is home to our lawnmowers, various pieces of equipment, assorted junk, and an underground conspiracy—masterminded by Guido Groundhog. Oh, sure, he appears to be a cute, cuddly fur ball of a creature, but in reality, he's a dirty, rotten, underhanded scoundrel. A wolf in sheep's clothing. Guido burrows beneath the earth, forming a strategic network of tunnels. His plan? Destroy the foundation of our house and garage. Swallow us all up into his little underground world. He is nasty!

To put an end to his evil plot, my husband Steve borrowed a live trap. We would outsmart this double-crossing critter. After consulting Punxsutawney Phil and watching the movie *Groundhog Day* fifteen times, we mapped out the precise spot to set the trap. Guido would take his midnight stroll, poke his head up through the soil, be enticed by the lovely array of crisp greens, and follow his nose right into the snare. Perfect.

Steve checked the trap periodically, only to be disappointed. Then one day as he opened the garage door he observed movement. Black-and-white movement. Upon closer examination, Steve realized it was Oreo, our oversized "elephant" cat. She had escaped from the house, discovered the underground maze, and fallen for our fail-proof scheme. Stupid cat! We were now assured the plan worked; it was just a matter of time. We would play the waiting game.

Another day. Steve lifted the garage door. Movement. Black-and-white movement. Tail up. Aghhh! It's a skunk! The garage door closed faster than a sneeze, with Steve hot-trotting away in a full-blown tizzy.

Now the question was *What do we do?* We can't just leave it there. Animal control—that's the answer! Steve called. Apparently, animal control couldn't handle this type of situation but gave Steve the names and phone numbers of a few people who could. With each phone call, he got an answering machine and left a message. No one called back. The chickens!

Later that afternoon we went to church for a wedding open house. The interview process began. We told everyone there of our crisis and asked, "What would you do?" We didn't get any good or realistic advice. We got "If it dies in the trap, it will spray." "If you shoot it, it will spray." "If you go near it, it will spray." "If you whisper sweet nothings in its ear, it will spray." "If you blast it with carbon monoxide, it will spray."

After returning home, Steve scoured the neighborhood for advice. Same old thing. We were in a hopeless situation. We had to figure out something in a hurry. We could not live with the consequences of a spraying skunk. Our attached garage warehoused product for our vending company. Our house is a step away. The results would be repulsive.

After much thought and careful consideration, Steve devised a plan. He stationed our son, Ryan, in the yard, a good distance away but close enough to verbally guide his dad's movements. Steve fashioned a long, stiff wire with a hooked end and cautiously climbed onto the garage roof. He was prone and precarious as he dangled over the edge and dropped the wire in an attempt to hook the handle of the garage door. With Ryan's supervision and Steve's great concentration, the connection was made. The idea was to raise the door, reach inside the garage with the wire, and lift the trap door, allowing the skunk (and us) freedom. Slowly, gently, the garage door glided up the tracks. Before it reached the halfway point, Ryan hollered, "Dad! Dad! It's not a skunk, it's a possum!" Duh!

I don't know if he slept through Animal Recognition 101 or what, but where I come from skunks and possums are as different as pigs and alligators. This was a clear-cut case of mistaken identity. It's also a case of letting the imagination go wild, thinking the worst, and getting all worked up over nothing. On the brighter side, it certainly gave us an entertaining story to tell. (For Steve's sake, I'm convinced that God miraculously changed the skunk into a possum.)

Remember the biblical account in Numbers 13 and 14 when Moses sent twelve men into Canaan to explore the land? They were told to check out everything—the people, towns, soil, trees, fruit. After forty days, they returned with their report. "The land is wonderful! It does flow with milk and honey! The fruit is magnificent! *But*, the land is crawling with skunks. Big skunks. We can't do anything about them. It is a hopeless situation."

Joshua and Caleb, two of the spies, couldn't stay quiet. "Wait a minute, here. The land is exceedingly good, and if the Lord is pleased with us, He'll give it to us. We don't need to be afraid of the skunks, because the Lord is with us. He can change the skunks into possums."

Joshua and Caleb had great faith. Their eyes were fixed on God. The assembly of people was enraged. They were determined to think the worst and they focused on the smell of the skunks. The result? Forty more years of wandering in the wilderness. Their lack of faith caused them to miss out on the Promised Land.

We have lots of life situations that appear as skunks to us. Our imaginations tend to run wild and we worry needlessly, when in reality the problem is a case of mistaken identity. Before your circumstances leave you feeling hopeless, fix your eyes on God. He can turn your skunks into possums. Take it from someone who knows.

But my eyes are fixed on You, O Sovereign Lord; in You I take refuge. (Psalm 141:8a)

In a Fix

I was in a fix. I had just fixed lunch, downed a cup of coffee for my caffeine fix, and was fixin' to go pick up my clock that got fixed, but my recently fixed dog was causing such a ruckus that I couldn't fix my attention on my plans. I'm gonna have to fix that.

Have you ever noticed that some words have multiple meanings? I hadn't given the word "fix" much thought until looking in the dictionary and seeing one definition after another. That put me in a fix, because I had to determine which meaning was appropriate for my need.

To be in a fix is like being in a predicament or a bind, or in my case a strange, off-the-wall situation that nobody in her right mind would ever think of doing. I'm almost embarrassed to tell this; it was certainly a brainless blunder, something I'll never be allowed to forget. Summer was drawing to an end—August 24. *My, that date sure rings a bell for me,* I thought on and off as I went about my business. Later in the day, I glanced at a piece of paper in a pile and suddenly realized why that date was so familiar. It happened to be the first day of school and I had forgotten to take my kids! I realized my irrevocable mistake one hour before school was to be dismissed. Do you know how idiotic I felt when I called the school and confessed my airheadedness? How could something like this happen? Hadn't we just ended a grueling summer, the kids driving me crazy, and me more than excited for school to start? When my shocked friends laughed at me and asked how any mother could do such a thing, I merely stated that I love my kids way too much and wanted them home an extra day. (For some reason they didn't believe me.) Anyhow, the principal fixed it so I wouldn't repeat my folly. The next year I was assigned responsibilities for the first day of classes. Fixed that fix!

Have you ever wondered why we fix lunch when it was never broken? This particular wording means to prepare, not repair; though there might be times you're headed to the table with piping hot bowls of scrumpdillyicious food when you trip over your toddler's toy, dropping everything and splattering food and dishes from here to Timbuktu. In this instance, you would need to fix the fixin's.

Why do we get dogs and cats fixed? One time Max, the wonder dog, hurt his leg, causing him to limp. We took Max to the vet to see if he could get fixed. You have to be careful when talking to vets about fixing your animals, though. They might get the wrong idea. Evidently fixing your animals has more than one meaning. On that note, I'm fixin' to go on to the next thing, which makes me ask— what's with fixin' to go somewhere? I'm stumped when trying to figure out how this means you're getting ready to go. Maybe I should interview a southerner. And then, how does a caffeine fix fix us? I find I have more questions the longer I ponder the word.

I recently learned what keeping your eyes fixed means, and I didn't learn it from an ophthalmologist. I experienced it first hand when driving home during a severe winter storm. I was in Michigan with my daughter Laney for a funeral and was planning to stay a few extra days if needed. Then the weather reports grew glum. The weathermen were advising of a winter storm warning throughout the entire Midwest. The report from Iowa was that seven and a half inches of snow had fallen and gusty winds were coming in. The storm was heading straight for Michigan and that didn't sound good at all. I certainly didn't want to be holed up in Michigan away from my family for who knows how long. I was in a fix. I didn't know what to do. I was planning to bring my niece and nephew home with me for a few days until their parents came through to pick them up. It was a tough decision, but I chose to leave right away and try to outrun the weather coming my way. After promising my brother we would stay in a hotel if the weather got too bad, we headed off toward Iowa.

As we left, the snow hit and hit hard. The frozen fluffy stuff came down like cats and dogs. (Fixed ones, of course! In fact, I think there were some puppies and kittens thrown in there, too.) A world of white was all we could see. The highway blended with the surrounding fields. My little Mazda plodded along with the rest of traffic as I tried to position myself directly behind a semi with hopes it would lead the way and make the path for me. We passed numerous vehicles in the ditch. The roads were near impassable. I was thankful for the chatter of the kids that helped keep me encouraged and my brain engaged. "Don't ever try to do this," I warned them.

Determination got us to the Interstate 80 exit where we got a bite to eat and considered our options. After eating, taking a potty break, and making a quick call to Iowa, we decided to carefully continue tunneling our way home. Patches of our new highway seemed a tad better, but as we progressed it got worse. Blustery winds created snow drifts across the road, until eventually the interstate flow slowed to the pace of turtle herd. My eyes were riveted to the road. They didn't turn to the right or to the left. I didn't let anything or anyone distract me from my straight-ahead course. My focus was on our destination—home. A normally four-and-a half-hour trip turned into seven-plus hours. I could have become weary and given up, but I inched forward, knowing that each mile was one mile closer to home. I kept my goal in view and my eyes were so fixed, or concentrated, on what I was doing that I couldn't think about anything else.

I believe God gave me this experience to illustrate the importance of keeping our eyes fixed on Him. Many times we have "winter weather" in our lives that causes us to get distracted. We get sidetracked and can't focus our attention on anyone or anything but the problems at hand. Then the more we focus on the problems and distractions, the more we start to slide into a negative bent. We lose sight of our goal and, therefore, our hope.

If we could slip on the sandals of some of our Bible heroes we would realize that they traveled through many severe storms with eyes riveted, not on the weather but on God. They were on the highway of holiness with heaven as their destination, and they didn't give up. Joseph had family problems. Moses had an overwhelming job. David was on the run from Saul for years and was even tempted to retaliate at times. Abraham was tested over and over again.

Our situations today are as difficult for us as the ones we read about in the Bible. I'm happy God preserved these and other stories for us, because they all serve as reminders that God can and will see us through. When our biblical friends weathered their trying circumstances successfully, their eyes were fixed on God. They looked ahead, beyond their situations, to their future, and zeroed in. They didn't look to the right or to the left. They didn't get sidetracked. They lived onward and upward lives. The faith and trust they had in the One who created them let them see things from God's viewpoint, allowing them to rest in His big but gentle arms.

The more they rested in God's arms, the more they personally knew His character. The more they knew God's character, the more they trusted Him. The more they trusted God, the more they could see Him work. The more they could see God work, the more they reverenced Him. The more they reverenced Him, the more they lived their lives in a state of worship—not just Sundays, but every day. The more they worshiped, the more they delighted in God, and pretty soon the winter weather just didn't matter anymore. See the progression?

Fixing our eyes on Jesus involves trust. It is an attitude of faith. It is looking beyond the problems of today and toward the future, knowing that God has everything in control and knowing that nothing comes into our lives without His concern and His provision.

Because of what Christ did for us on the cross, we have a hope set before us. If we live for that future hope, we will be enabled to endure. As we get to know Him through the Word and yield to His Spirit He increases our faith and helps us to keep on truckin' no matter the weather.

Are you in a fix? Then worship God and find rest in His loving arms.

Therefore, since we are surrounded by such a great cloud of witnesses, let us throw off everything that hinders and the sin that so easily entangles, and let us run with perseverance the race marked out for us. Let us fix our eyes on Jesus, the author and perfecter of our faith, who for the joy set before Him endured the cross, scorning its shame, and sat down at the right hand of the throne of God. (Hebrews 12:1–2)

Big Honkin' Words

As I write this I am awake, alert, and lucid, in no apparent distress. My wounds, if I had any, are well healed without evidence of erythema or drainage. My skin is dry and I am not diaphoretic. I have a normal gait and station and ambulate without any hint of antalgia, other than when I have a catch in my giddyup. I can walk on my tiptoes and heels without difficulty. Sensation, strength, and reflexes are grossly intact, as well as cranial nerves, except for some intermittent senility that tends to run rampant at times. (It's that over-forty thing!) I am oriented to person, place, and time (usually). I can spell "world" forwards and backwards, but I can't remember what happened five minutes ago or where I've put my car keys; so, I'd have to say that my recent and remote memory appears shaky at times. I occasionally suffer from expressive aphasia and emotional incontinence, too. At this point, I do not have a clear-cut radiculopathy or paresthesia extending anywhere. Additionally, a myelopathy, hemangiopericytoma, spondylolisthesis,

29

and lots of other twenty-five cent words can be crossed off the list of things I don't have, although I do have a good case of blood in my veins. Unfortunately, however, my husband has an ongoing problem with cranial alopecia, for which a cure has not been found!

One of the blessings for me over the past couple of years has been a job that God miraculously dropped in my lap—medical transcribing for a group of neurosurgeons. It has helped sharpen my mind, something I desperately needed after having a baby. (I was told by a reliable source that when you're pregnant you lose brain cells. It takes two years after giving birth to start regaining them. After my little man turned two, first I celebrated, then I went into a daily routine of measuring my head to see if I could notice a day-to-day difference. I really do think there is some truth to this concept. If nothing else, it gave me a thread of hope.) But the best thing of all about this kind of work is that I've learned some big honkin' words that make me sound incredibly intelligent. Plus, I think pretty soon I'll be qualified to do brain surgery. It's an at-home-learn-as-you-go program. Anybody want to be my first patient?

I have typed for five doctors, who all say things in their own way. I get a kick out of their descriptions of patients at times. If Mr. Patient is somewhat large, Dr. H might describe him as morbidly obese. Dr. M might say the same patient is moderately overweight. Then Dr. T might leave the report as saying the patient has a normal body habitus. I know if I had my druthers about which doctor to see it would be the last one.

Dr. M is from a foreign country. His dictation tends to be very interesting when the medical terminology is combined with his thick accent. I have to be oh-so-careful about figuring out what he is saying; otherwise, the poor patient might end up being near death on paper when in reality he only had something like a hangnail. If a phrase is overly familiar to Dr. P, he says it faster than I can blink in a runtogethermumbledfashion. Dr. R is very soft spoken and talks quietly on the tapes. I really have to hone in with my new brain cells to decipher the doctor lingo properly.

I have a tidbit that might be of interest to you. With all the medical reports I've typed so far, not one has mentioned the patient having holey or dirty underwear. So, all you mothers out there who have instilled in your children that they should always change their underwear because they never know when they'll be in an accident or need to go to the doctor or hospital—keep up the fine work!

Some of these big honkin' words can be fun to play with. I told my friend Rick that he was diaphoretic, so he thought he should get as much sympathy from others as he could. "Oh, honey, I can't take out the garbage. I'm diaphoretic." "Could you please get me a drink? I can't move. I've got that diaphoretic thing going on." "Dear, would you feed me my grapes one by one and fan the air gently around me? I'm becoming quite weak, because, as you know, I'm diaphoretic." I could tell right away that I must warn Nancy, Rick's wife, that his "disease" was nothing a little antiperspirant or cool shower couldn't fix.

Dr. H once described an elderly gentleman as being loquacious. *Now that's an interesting word,* I thought. I typed it, even got it spelled correctly, but didn't find the word in the medical dictionary. My curiosity was aroused. I looked it up in my trusty old Webster's and found that this word would describe my daughter, a friend or two of mine, and, believe it or not, me once in a while. I was determined to use my newfound word several times that week, and I did. Boy, I'm hot stuff now! What's really neat is that I actually know a big word, can use it properly in a sentence, and can tell somebody what it means. Does it seem to you that I talk excessively? Just wondering.

I sometimes question why doctors have to use huge fifteen- or sixteen-letter words that don't make any sense to anybody, when a four- or five-letter word would suffice. Maybe they figure that since they spent all that money on their education they need to sound smart. Who knows? I could let them in on a little secret, though. If they used shorter words, I wouldn't have to type as much and they'd save money. On second thought, I think I'll keep that secret to myself.

All this talk about big honkin' words reminds me of Someone else who has some real doozies. I've noticed through the years that God's huge words could fill page after page, and I'm daily experiencing the depth of their meaning. For example: I AM. I know those appear to be two little bitty words that consist of a total of three letters, but within those three letters is the biggest, most power-packed message you will ever find. When God says "I AM," He is saying: "I am sufficient. I am faithful. I am the God of details. I am the God of the impossible. I am always with you. I am your equipper. I am your provider. I am your strength. I am your shield. I am your hiding place. I am your all in all. I am love. I am life. Besides that, I am all-knowing, and I am all-powerful. I Am Who I Am." The wonderful thing to notice here is that He says, "I AM." Right now. Always present. Today. With God time makes no difference in who He is, was, or will be. These are words He spoke several millenniums ago to our biblical heroes. These are words He speaks to us today.

As we forge into this new millennium, I plan to continue relying on and trusting in the God who calls Himself "I Am Who I Am." I plan to get to know Him even better and fall more deeply in love with Him. Will you make that your goal today and in the years ahead? Get your eyes fixed. Put your trust in God. Put your hope in God. Allow yourself to experience His character more fully. Read your Bible and savor what it says. Pray. I guarantee the more you seek Him out, the more you'll understand and be able to incorporate His big honkin' words. Shalom!

I Am Who I Am. . . . This is My name forever, the name by which I am to be remembered from generation to generation. (Exodus 3:14,15)

Reproducing

Rabbits multiply. Aren't you glad I let you in on that little secret? I once read that we have Easter bunnies because bunnies are prolific. They symbolize new life, and new life is what Christ gives us as a result of His death and resurrection.

I collect rabbits and have ever since the years I dated my husband Steve. Steve's nickname at the time was Rabbit. Not because he's always in a hurry or is fast. He's one of the most laid-back guys a person could ever meet. His name came as a result of a haircut that his friends claimed made him look like a turtle. They dubbed him Turtle. Well, Steve didn't exactly care for that title, so they started calling him Rabbit instead. Kind of crazy, but it stuck.

As I reminisce about our wedding day, I fondly recall the gold rabbit necklace I wore with my fancy gown. Rabbits decorated the table in front of our cake, and we even served our guests rabbit-shaped mints! Our plans were to name our children Bunny, Jack, and Peter.

Today, only on rare instances is Steve ever called Rabbit, and it's usually by people who haven't seen him for years. So, with each day he's becoming less and less of a Rabbit. He's becoming less and less of a hare. He's becoming a man with less and less hair!

I have rabbits all over the house. I've watched my collection multiply over the years. There's the floppy-eared, floppy-bodied variety. Handmade. Quilted. Stuffed. Wooden. Cross-stitched. Goofy-faced. Big. Small. You name it; we've got it! Each rabbit reminds me of the special friend or family member who gave it to me, or it brings back a fun memory. Looking at them fills me with warm and happy thoughts.

Years ago when we lived in our first house we displayed our assorted rabbits in a spare bedroom. We lovingly referred to this room as "the bunny room." My piano, loaded with the treasures, stood against the wall. When the time came to replace the carpet in the room, we ripped out the old green and yellow shag, which exposed white squares of linoleum flooring. Much to our astonishment, one lonely square tile imprinted with Bugs Bunny's picture lay in the spot directly under the piano, where the bulk of our bunnies were. What a shock! God had sprung quite a surprise on us and we giggled in joy as we pictured Him smiling down from heaven. I kept that unique tile to remind us of our great God who blesses us in unimaginable ways.

Much as rabbits reproduce—the live kind and the collectible kind—we, too, are supposed to reproduce. Don't worry; I'm not going to go into a full-blown explanation of how reproduction works. I'd get way too embarrassed and turn bright red and start sweating and all that stuff. Besides, I'm not talking just about babies here. But I'll give you a little tidbit to chew on. We can't reproduce on our own. It takes our connectedness with another.

Have you ever noticed that the longer you're with someone, the more you become like him or her? (It's kind of like dogs and their owners. Isn't it funny how much they resemble each other?) You pick up the person's habits, their pattern of speech, their likes, and dislikes. You might even catch yourself finishing their sentences or thinking the exact same thought at the exact same time. This happens with husbands and wives a lot. That's because intimacy breeds reproduction. (Wow! Ponder on that one for a while!) It's true in the physical sense, it's true in the social sense, and it's true in the spiritual sense.

God wants us to imitate Him, to reproduce the qualities seen in His Son. How? By remaining in Him. By spending so much time with Him that He "rubs off" on us. By getting to know Him so well and loving Him so much that we can't think of doing anything else but pleasing Him. The more connected we are to Christ, the more we will bear Christ-like fruit.

It doesn't stop there, though. The more we bear Christ-like fruit, the more people take notice. The more people take notice, the more they see Christ at work in us. The more they see Christ in us, the more they are drawn to Him. The more they are drawn to Him, the more they want to give their lives over to Christ. The result is more people remaining in Christ and more people reproducing Christ-like fruit. Isn't it amazing how this works? It goes on and on and on and on and on. Just like the Energizer Bunny.

Speaking of bunnies again, let's hop to it and reproduce. Know what I mean?

Remain in Me, and I will remain in you. No branch can bear fruit by itself; it must remain in the vine. Neither can you bear fruit unless you remain in Me. (John 15:4)

Tight Spots

Have you ever been in a tight spot? I've been in a few.

Years ago, for various reasons, my husband and I discarded our king-size waterbed and temporarily down-sized to our original marriage bed, a bed with a full-size mattress. It didn't take long for us both to realize that the bed had shrunk since we first used it. We found, through several death-defying escapades of nearly falling out of bed, that we had to choreograph our attempts at sleeping. So, each night when hitting the hay we both started out facing stage right. At precisely the stroke of midnight, we rolled over, in unison, to stage left. Two hours later, in one fluid motion, we were on our backs at center stage. Then Steve started snoring. I kicked him repeatedly until he was stage right again, with me not far behind. This pattern continued throughout the night and into the morning, when our alarm clock halted the synchronized snoozing. If either of us made one false move or dared breathe at the wrong time, it was all over. Steve, verbal artist that he is, described our new sleeping arrangements to our amused friends as being like "two hot dogs in one bun." (Yes, it was a tight spot for us, but we now have a king-size bed again and are forever grateful!)

I've experienced some tight spots in my car, too, because of a combination of modern technology and hoop earrings. Picture this: I'm sitting in the driver's seat minding my own business. I pull into a parking place, turn off the ignition, open the door, and voila! The next thing I know is that I'm practically standing on my head underneath the steering wheel. Is it magic? No, it's that the new-fangled sliding-in-the-door-panel seat belts latched onto my earring and took my head and the rest of me for a ride. I found my noggin stuck between the steering wheel and the dashboard. What a tight spot! And a position that is quite humorous to onlookers, I'm sure. Unfortunately, I have repeated this fiasco more than once. I've got to remember that it's dangerous to dangle and drive at the same time.

Another situation causing me great duress in the car was the bag-in-the-lap trick. While driving with one hand and foraging through my purse with another, I somehow managed to wrap my purse strap around the steering wheel several times. While trying to proceed after having stopped at a red light, I noticed my steering wheel was stuck. We're talking that it wouldn't move to the right or to the left. This was quite a predicament—one that caused panic—especially since I was in the center lane of a busy highway with cars zooming around me on both sides. I found it nearly impossible to navigate my car, but after some intense pleas to God for help, I eventually pulled to a safe stop. God was probably giggling as I unwound the leather strap, and I was thinking that only I could possibly do something quite that strange. Yes, a typical Twila tight spot.

My little man, Jesse, needlessly lived through a tight spot brought on by my husband. When I was caring for my other son, Ryan, in the hospital, I asked Steve to buy diapers because Jesse's supply was getting low. For some reason unknown to me and every other person on earth, Steve bought size twelve-to-eighteen diapers, but Jesse weighed thirty-two pounds. The poor guy got to know what close quarters were all about! His daddy didn't have much sympathy for the situation until I asked him how he would like to wear size small underwear on his extra-large body. But, with Steve being the good steward he is, Jesse wore every diaper in the package.

I sometimes feel as though I'm in a tight spot when I pull into the drive-through at Burger King and a voice asks for my order before I've made a decision. I break into a sweat, almost reaching full-blown hyperventilation, because I can't decide between the Whopper and pork tenderloin. Do you know how hard it is to pick a sandwich under that kind of pressure?

Speaking of sandwiches and extreme pressure, I think of Moses in one of his tight spots. At one point, he was the lettuce sandwiched between the hot mustard of the Israelites and Pharaoh's baloney. Approaching Pharaoh on behalf of the Israelite nation, Moses said, "Lettuce go into the desert to offer sacrifices to the Lord our God." Pharaoh, full of baloney, spouted off that he didn't know their God and he greatly increased the Israelites' work load. The Israelites were hot (mustard, if you will).

"What's with you, Moses? You make us stink to Pharaoh. You were supposed to rescue us, but you've only caused more trouble!"

Moses was in a real pickle. He immediately went to ketchup with God and said, "Lord, I'm just a poor boy in a very tight spot. Why did you bring me here in the first place?" The Lord repeatedly assured Moses and continued to give needed direction. The rest is history.

At times in our lives, we are faced with tight spots, not necessarily like the ones I mentioned earlier, but some really tough issues. Maybe we're staring at a serious health problem or forced to make decisions that will affect the rest of our lives. Possibly our tight spot involves our kids and the route they are taking or a marital crisis. Perhaps it's whether or not to make a lifestyle change. When we are hit with certain circumstances we might feel caught in the middle. What do we do? Where do we go? How do we respond?

Moses did the right thing. He was in a real bind, but instead of sitting and stewing, he went straight to the Lord with his predicament. We can learn from his example. God will give us assurance and the direction we need if we leave our problems in His hands and act on His commands.

Cast your cares on the Lord and He will sustain you; He will never let the righteous fall. (Ps. 55:22)

The StraightWay Experience

Straightway. The word means at once or immediately. It's also what John the Baptist did. He made straight the way of the Lord. Compare this to what highway construction workers do. Their job is to clear obstructions or obstacles from a path to make the way clear so that others can go forward. John the Baptist was in the desert preparing the way for the Lord and His kingdom by calling on people to return to Him. John the Baptist came as a witness to testify concerning the Light.

StraightWay was a Christian bookstore my husband and I owned for nine years. We opened it when our son Ryan was two and our daughter Laney was a baby. StraightWay was a big part of all our lives.

StraightWay was instantly birthed. We never planned on having a Christian bookstore; it just happened. God miraculously opened the doors within six weeks of the idea being conceived in our minds.

The name came about in similar fashion. The Lord planted it in my husband's head, and when the day came to appoint it, StraightWay was the choice. Little did we know the name's significance at that time or that the Bible was full of straightways. God knew, though.

We were filled with a sense of excitement and adventure as friends joined us to prepare "our baby" for its arrival. Every detail was lovingly attended to. The walls were painstakingly painted and stenciled. The display pieces spruced up and handled with care. Every little thing mattered, because it was God's.

Over the years, StraightWay grew. Relationships were formed. Lives were changed. We were, in a sense, like a Christian bartender as our customers spilled their guts to us over the sales counter. We shared the joys and sorrows of those who walked through the doors: marriages, births, deaths, divorce. We began to know our customers by name. We remembered the products they purchased. Many of them were more than just customers; they became our friends.

With great rejoicing, we offered guidance to new Christians as they selected their first Bibles. We hand picked greeting cards, books, and music to suit our customer's needs. Tools for sharing the Gospel or for providing encouragement and enriching their Christian walk were available to help them.

Because of one of the videos we rented out, an abortion process was halted. We saw pictures of the precious child brought into the world as a result. Because of the Vacation Bible School and Sunday school curriculum we sold, countless children came to know the Lord in a personal way. Because of the accompaniment cassettes and musical cantatas people purchased from us, songs performed in church touched stubborn hearts that a sermon couldn't reach. I could go on and on with stories of changed lives as a result of the products we sold. What an honor to be in an industry that pointed people to our Savior and brought others into a closer relationship with Him!

There were other highlights and memories as well. We had a great friendship with our local Christian radio station and invited the deejays to join us for many of our celebrations via live remote. My husband and I voiced crazy radio ads. People came in just to see who those wackos, Steve and Twila, were. For a time, our names were synonymous with StraightWay.

Occasionally Christian recording artists visited us for autograph parties. Larnelle Harris, Whiteheart, Ray Boltz, and Twila Paris were just a few. Naturally, when Twila came, we had some fun with our names. We had a Twyla (she couldn't quite get the spelling right) working for us, too. We became the *Trilas*. Each of us wore a nametag to prevent confusion. (Have you ever heard me sing?) Even a customer named Twila joined in the frivolity. If I had thought of it sooner, I would have hung a banner over the door announcing, "You are now entering the Twila Zone." It was a blast! Twila Paris wore her nametag to the concert that night and shared our story with the audience.

For several years, we sponsored a "God is Awesome" party. Our alternative to trick-or-treating transformed the interior of our mall, providing a positive and safe environment for the many kids and parents who attended. Each year the attendance grew until we were bursting at the seams.

I remember the day a customer came to the counter after using our restroom and let us know how StraightWay had changed her life. "I was in your store two years ago and used the restroom then. It was there I was introduced to quilted toilet paper." Imagine that! Her life got a softer touch because of us. She's never been the same!

Many of our sales reps became our friends. We looked forward to their appointments and the times we fellowshipped at conventions. After we were involved in a motor vehicle accident, we received stacks of cards. Several of our reps visited us at home while I recovered. Some sent plants. "Leonard" is a plant I received from our card rep, Leonard. I tried to kill it off (like all my other plants), but today "Leonard" is strong and thriving, serving as a reminder of Leonard.

Yes, we had many good times. We have many memories. We witnessed many changed lives. But eventually the financial pressures mounted and the stress became unbearable. It was time—time to close this nine-year chapter in our lives.

I can't begin to define the heart-wrenching pain and the mental anguish we experienced. The process was like a funeral that lasted forever. We watched those years of hard work and sleepless nights go out the door. In closing, we hoped to generate as much cash as possible to apply toward bills. We promised not to go bankrupt. Our goal was to pay off every company in time. Then, to add salt to our wounds, insensitive customers asked questions like, "What are you going to do with all the money you make from this big sale?" Oh, if they only knew. Our lives and our stomachs were twisted in knots.

How could this be? Why was this happening? During the StraightWay years my dad was taken from me, my mom was taken from me, and now StraightWay was dying—like the death of a child. My identity—who I thought I was—all gone.

In the midst of my grieving, the midst of my inner turmoil, wondering why, God brought a glimmer of light along my path. A special lady, whom we had just met, shared a message God had revealed to her for us. "You were there to fill a gap. Now God has something bigger and better for you to do."

How true the word "gap" was. The day after we were scheduled to close, another Christian store was preparing to open, less than a mile away. The lady's words were like a balm, offering peace, reminding us that God was in control. He was in control of our opening StraightWay, and now He was in control of our closing StraightWay.

I wish I could say life was peachy-keen after awhile, that I never thought about StraightWay again. But I can't. When you grieve something so deeply, it takes time. It's a process. It took well over three years to begin seeing things clearly again.

After closing StraightWay my vision was hazy. Clouded over. I couldn't remember the highlights or rejoice in them. I could only see the pain, the heartache, and the stress. I maybe even had a little bit of resentment tucked in there, too.

I thought of all the money we had dumped into StraightWay. I thought of what we could have bought with all the money we dumped into it. I thought of all the money we had taken from our vending company to help pay the bills, leaving our vending company hurting. I thought of the loans we had taken against our house and are still paying off. I thought of the retirement money we no longer had. I thought of how Steve and I never took a paycheck from StraightWay because it was our ministry. We paid others, but not ourselves. I thought of the companies we would be paying out of our pockets for years because we chose not to claim bankruptcy. I thought of that brainless person who had the nerve to ask what we were going to do with all the money we made. I started referring to God's store as the "Money Sucking Pit." Yes, I guess there was some resentment hiding in there. I hang my head in shame.

With time and God's help, I was able to shorten the name to "MSP." Then I progressed to calling it "that place." Now I can actually call it by name and not have piercing pains go up and down my spine. I've come a long way. Thank you, Lord!

God has taught me a lot of lessons about the StraightWay experience. "About that identity business, Twila. Your identity is not tied up in your parents or your store. Your identity is in Me. You are who you are because of Me. You are a child of the Most High God. I'm the only One you need."

"Yes, Lord, You."

Then He got my attention again. "Remember those products you sold, Twila? Many of them are still being used. The Bibles are being read; the songs are still sung. The woman continues to be happy with quilted toilet paper. Oh, and by the way, remember that baby saved from the abortion? She's growing up now and reading the Bible on her own. The store is still making an impact. Wasn't it worth it, Twila?"

"Yes, Lord, it was."

Yet another thump on the head from the Lord. "Hey, Twila, I got to thinking. Remember that industry you loved being a part of? The Christian booksellers industry? Well, guess what? You're on the other side of it now with your writing. Same industry, same people, different angle. You have an advantage over other new writers because you know the industry."

"Wow, Lord, I'm starting to see how all things work together for good."

Just when I thought I had learned everything I could from my StraightWay experience, the Lord bent down and whispered in my ear. "Twila, there's more to that StraightWay name than you'll ever know. Your whole life is to be a StraightWay experience. You are to have straightway obedience in regard to My commands. You are to make straight the way for the King. You are to walk the straight way. You are a witness for Me. Your life is to testify concerning Me. You are pointing the way to Christ's return. You are removing obstacles out of the path so the road is clear. Twila, StraightWay isn't a store. It isn't your identity. StraightWay is your life. It is your calling. Everything you do should reflect that."

"Whoa, Lord, that's deep! But I'm with You all the way. Thanks for bringing it to my attention."

Make straight the way for the Lord. (John 1:23b)

Fresh Dirt

Uh oh, I just got lost in thought, I have to be careful. Sometimes I can't find my way out again. While there, though, I came up with a set of questions to ponder. For instance . . .

I heard a local radio personality sharing a story of how a bag of grass seed in his garage showed evidence of mice activity. My question is what happens when mice eat grass seed? Do they turn into Chia Pets?

Then one day I drove by Red Lobster and saw their sign advertising bottomless crab legs. My reaction was glad relief, because I wouldn't have wanted crab legs with bottoms. Do crabs even have bottoms? I'm telling you, inquiring minds want to know!

And, of course, there are those nagging questions like how much deeper would the ocean be without sponges? What hair color do they put on the driver's license of a bald man? If psychiatric statistics say that one in four people is mentally ill, and my three friends are normal, what does

51

that say about me? Why does God let bad things happen to His people?

Whoa! Hold your horses! All of a sudden we're deep. But deeper yet was that pit into which a promising lad named Joseph was thrown. Joseph obediently went to check on his older brothers for his father. They were grazing the flocks in Shechem, a forty-five- to fifty-mile trip from home. Remember, they didn't have four-wheelers back then; he hoofed it. Once he got to Shechem, Joseph discovered that the group of shepherds had moved to Dothan, so he went above and beyond the call of duty and journeyed the extra twenty miles to get there.

When Joseph arrived, he wasn't exactly greeted enthusiastically. His brothers wouldn't win any awards for being a model welcoming committee. They didn't roll out the red carpet; instead they pulled the rug right out from under him! Acting out of larger-than-life jealousy, they plotted to kill him. Thanks to Reuben, they opted instead to throw him into a deep pit in the desert. Then, as if nothing was wrong, the brothers sat down to enjoy a lovely meal. When they looked up, they spotted a caravan heading to Egypt with a load of goods. So Joseph was pulled up from the pit and sold into slavery. He was taken to a far off land where he didn't know the people or the language. From one bad situation to another.

What's the deal here? Joseph was just being a good kid, obeying his father. One minute he's walking to Dothan, the next he's being carted off to Egypt. One minute he was a favored son, the next he's a forlorn slave. Why did God let this happen? Good question.

Joseph was sold to Potiphar, one of Pharaoh's high-ranking officials. The Bible tells us that the Lord was with Joseph; he prospered and was successful in everything he did. Then Potiphar's wife made up a farfetched fabrication that flung Joseph into prison. She was ticked off because he wouldn't have sexual relations with her. Joseph was extremely careful not to compromise his position, and now he was being punished. If God was with him in everything he did, how could He allow Joseph to suffer unjustly like this? Another good question.

All of this reminds me of the day I repotted Leonard, my scrawny, scraggly looking, and unhealthy plant. Leonard had definitely seen better days. I removed the small pot of dirt, shook the old dirt off, and noticed that the roots were all scrunched together. I selected a nice big pot and filled it with new soil. As I carefully placed Leonard in new surroundings, it was as though I heard, "Oh, boy! Fresh dirt!" The plant wiggled its roots around, and they spread out, firmly taking hold. God was allowing me to witness one of His little secrets: "It's the new dirt that allows Leonard to grow. Running out of room in the small pot was hampering the life process. With the big pot, Leonard's roots can run deep, solidly anchoring themselves. Leonard will now be sturdy and able to withstand a whole lot more." Today my plant is huge, healthy, and thriving, all because of fresh dirt.

Now back to Joseph. It seemed like he was constantly being thrown into "fresh dirt." What did he gain from it? Well, the story in Genesis goes on to tell how he was promoted from prisoner to prime minister, second only to Pharaoh. His years of being thrown into one challenging situation after another had prepared him to lead like no other. In fact, God knew years beforehand that Joseph would be the one to save his own nation from demise. Joseph anchored his roots firmly in the Lord. He grew in the dirt tossed his way and matured into a healthy, thriving, productive ruler.

Often we are faced with less than pleasant circumstances. Many times it seems we just get pulled out of one deep pit before we're thrown into another. We're up to our eyeballs in fresh dirt. We find ourselves asking, "Why did God let this happen? I've been obedient. I thought I was doing His will." You probably are.

Something I've discovered is that God uses unique methods for training His children. Maybe instead of asking "Why?" we should be saying, "I wonder what God has in store for me."

And we know that in all things God works for the good of those who love Him, who have been called according to His purpose. (Rom. 8:28)

Bad Days

You know you're having a bad day when you put on your bra backwards and it fits better! That's what the magnet announced, and I'd have to agree. I was drawn to the magnet and felt compelled to buy it, not because it applied to me, but because it was a message that needed to be shared. I gave it to a dear, frustrated friend. (Ain't I sweet?)

How about this? You know you're having a bad day when an acquaintance discreetly points out that your shoulder pad has slipped to your hip. This kind gesture is really appreciated until you realize your blouse doesn't have shoulder pads. Now, that's something I can relate to.

One of my favorite greeting cards tells a story of a young lad having a bad day. The picture on front is of a boy in an orange and yellow shirt, sitting at a table covered with a red and white-checkered cloth. An ice cream scoop is to his left, an orange sherbet container to his right. A bountiful bowl is positioned before him. The spoon in his left hand has just deposited the first bite of the frozen delicacy into his mouth. We see a look of contortion on his lime green face with lips puckered, bulging eyes the size of ping pong balls, and beads of perspiration popping from his pores. His vibrant orange-red hair stands at attention. The card tells how he went to the freezer and got out a bucket that said "Orange Sherbet" on top. He scooped a big bowlful, took a huge bite, and almost barfed! It wasn't orange sherbet after all. It was frozen chicken fat!

When you open the card you find the question, "Now doesn't that just brighten your whole life?"

Isn't that a great encouragement card? I only wish I had been the creative influence behind it. Can you picture that happening? It tends to give me a whole new outlook on my annoyances. Just think; it could have been me salivating for this citrusy sweet, my taste buds doing the tango in anticipation of that flavor-filled first bite. And, it could have been my cheeks packed with icicle-laden, greasy-grossy poultry globules. Yum, yum! Maybe that bad hair day I was having wasn't so bad after all!

The Apostle Paul experienced a bad day or two. Let's get real here. He had enough bad days in just a few short years to last most of us three or four lifetimes. He attracted bad days like we attract mosquitoes. In fact, he had a degree in it: Apostle Paul, M.B.D.—Master of Bad Days. What makes him so unique, though, is that he knew how to handle them. Somehow, he had the gift of looking at his rotten predicaments and catastrophic calamities as opportunities for God to work. He saw the bright side of these daily ordeals and, believe it or not, was even thankful and rejoiced in them. Boy, some of us have a long way to go, don't we?

On one particular occasion, Paul was imprisoned in Rome. His new accommodations weren't exactly a five-star luxury suite, either. He stayed in a dark and dreary dung hole, infested with furry friends, without even a treadmill or television to entertain him. On top of that, he was chained to a Roman soldier twenty-four hours a day, with shift changes every six hours.

Paul could have blown a fuse, dropkicked his rat roommates in rage, and slung his stale bread and lukewarm water against the dank dungeon walls. He could have stormed up and down while furiously beating his chest, thundering, "Why me? I'm not scheduled for another bad day until March 15th three years from now!" But, no. Good old Paul smelled an opportunity brewing. With his great mathematical mind, he calculated that four guards would be connected to him each day. He knew a "captive" audience when he saw one. Little did his shackled chaperones know, but they were in for a shock! Did Paul keep his mouth shut? No way! I can just imagine him thinking, "What can they do, throw me in prison? Chain me? Beat me? Been there, done that." He had nothing to lose, so Paul didn't hold back. He seized the moment and gave it all he had. The prison police didn't have a chance!

Because he made the most of his "bad hair day," he was able to get the Gospel into the elite Praetorian Guard and to the officials in Caesar's court. Paul discovered that his circumstances really opened up new areas of ministry for him. We see why he could tell the Philippians in his letter that these major setbacks actually served to advance the Gospel. Apart from Jesus Christ Himself, there was no one who shaped the history of Christianity like Paul. Wow! What a contrast from looking at things with a negative mindset!

Let's backtrack a little bit now and review our bad days. Maybe we can find a bright side and improve our perspective.

The bra that fit better backwards? This is great! You can get twice as much wear from it. When it's worn out on one side, flip it around and wear it the other way. Think of the money you'll save!

The shoulder pad that supposedly slipped, but didn't? Do you know how many starving people in China would give anything to have hips like ours? We can also be thankful for the little extra cushion when sitting on those hard bleachers at baseball games.

The bad hair day? Perhaps there's a new career in clowning ahead. After all, Bozo needs a buddy. The possibilities are endless: in-home birthday parties, restaurants, and circuses. Our hair could reach new heights in making people happy!

The frozen chicken fat? Just think of the chicken gravy we can make! Or, you know, all those vitamin pills I take sure seem to slide down easier these days! Actually, though, think of all the money that crazy guy is making by sharing his bad day experience with us in a greeting card!

Yes, I'm aware that these all sound silly, but what does it hurt to view our unfavorable conditions from an amusing angle? The way we react to our adversities might in itself be a way to advance the Good News. People will definitely notice our overcoming attitude and therefore could be drawn to Christ. Let's turn our negatives into positives and see what God can do. I'm willing to give it a try. How about you?

Rejoice in the Lord always. I will say it again: Rejoice!
(Phil. 4:4)

Whatever, Lord!

No, I can't, Lord!"

"Yes, you can, Twila."

"No, I can't, Lord!"

"Yes, you can, Twila."

"But, Lord, how can I write when I don't even know how to talk?"

"Trust Me."

"Okay, Lord, this is the deal then: I'll hold the pen; You do the rest."

"It's a deal."

I'm so glad God never gives us a job to do without equipping us first. There are many times I feel like a Moses; I just can't do what God is asking. I'm not competent. Then God reminds me that He doesn't want competence, He wants obedience. Something I try to remember when I have my "Moses moments" is that God never calls the equipped; He equips the called. Well, that's how I got this little writing project. Obedience. I couldn't get out of it. So, if you don't like the book, you can talk to my Higher Authority.

Shortly after submitting to God, I pled, "Lord, give me what other writers have." Later, I looked in the mirror, and there, protruding from my chin was a one-inch hair. I knew at that point I had achieved writer's status, because I had recently read books by three different authors referring to their chin hairs. See, God does answer prayer! I wonder if the length or quantity of chin hairs is directly related to the quality of the writer's work. If so, I've seen some pretty gifted writers in my day. I think I'll run and check the mirror again!

A while back, I attended my first writer's conference at Wheaton College in Wheaton, Illinois. A great opportunity with perfect timing, made available by none other than God Himself. It was a special time of learning about this thing called writing and a chance to chat with real live writers, authors, and editors. After the first day (Monday), I prayed for circumstances to present themselves to meet one-on-one with the woman teaching my daily class. She is an author and editor and was also the keynote speaker scheduled for the Thursday night banquet.

Before going to this conference, I purchased a small travel alarm clock. I set it to wake me up each morning at about 5:30. Monday and Tuesday mornings I arose well before the alarm clock clanged, or the rooster crowed for that matter. (After all, mornings and me are like two peas in a pod. Yeah, right! Actually, in the mornings I'm usually more like the earth at its beginnings—formless and void.)

Wednesday morning, however, was another story. I awakened to the loudest, most obnoxious noise I'd heard since leaving my kids behind at home. The sound was like a foghorn or a goose honking over a loud speaker, amplified thirty times. Immediately I responded by turning off my alarm clock. I thought, *Wow! This is the loudest alarm clock I've ever heard. Pretty amazing for something so small!* After turning on the light in my room and noticing that the blast was ongoing, I looked at the clock. Four A.M. Along with the noise came intermittent flashing lights. With my partially engaged brain I realized this was something out of the ordinary. It must be a fire alarm.

I grabbed my robe and slippers and trudged down the stairs and outside with all the other men and women. (I was glad I bought a robe before I went. Otherwise, it wouldn't have been a pretty sight.) Now, as I stood across the street from the dormitory listening to the deafening sound, watching the flashing-light display in the windows, hearing the fire trucks roaring toward us, and seeing the firemen roam throughout the building, the circumstances I had prayed about presented themselves.

Standing next to me in the crisp, cool air, groggy-eyed and in her pajamas, was Sandy, the one I asked God to arrange a meeting with. Not one to pass up an opportunity (after all, the Bible says to make the most of every opportunity), I told Sandy I had prayed for the chance to talk with her—and look, here we were! I don't think she was too amused at God's timing. In fact, during her little talk at the banquet Thursday night, she said, "Twila, next time you pray about meeting an editor or someone else, be more specific with your request." I love the way God works. He cracks me up! The fire alarm was just a fluke, but God certainly proved once again that He answers prayer.

Not too long after I finally accepted that God wanted me to write, He made something else clear to me.

"Twila, I want you to be a speaker."

"Uh, God, do You remember that excuse I gave You for not writing? Let me refresh Your memory. It went like this— How can I write when I can't even talk? Lord, You do know that in order to be a speaker a person must first know how to talk, don't You?"

"Well, Twila, let me remind you of the time I used the mouth of a donkey to get My message across. If I can use a donkey, I can surely use you, can't I?"

"I guess You're right, Lord. But what if I goof up royally and look like a big twit?"

"It's not about you, Twila."

Ah, yes! That's something I always need to remember. It's not about me. It's about Him. God doesn't need my help. He can get the job done with me or without me. But He chose me to carry out this particular work so that I might be blessed. And, believe it or not, God can be glorified by using a donkey like me.

Obedience to God involves taking risks and moving us beyond our comfort zone. It's what I call "life on the edge." You never know what's on the other side, but it sure makes for an exciting ride. It seems like I'm getting a lot of opportunities for obedience lately. I've learned that God always comes through with His end of the deal. When God tells me to do something and I do it in obedience, He provides a way to make it happen. I'm getting to the point that I can pretty much say, "Whatever, Lord!" and know that He's going to take care of the details.

Now, back to this book. God wanted me to write it, so I'm doing it. I won't try to get out of it.

"But what if people laugh at me?"

"That's what you want, isn't it, Twila?"

"Who's going to read it anyway?"

"Don't worry about it, Twila."

"Lord, what about a publisher? It doesn't get read if it's not published."

"Knock it off, Twila. Don't I know these things? I'm God. Aren't I enough?"

"Okay, Lord—whatever."

I don't know all the answers. I can't see the big picture. God has something planned for my future that I can't comprehend right now. But as long as I remember that God knows, and as long as I remember how big God is, I'm fine. There's no better place to be than in the center of His will. God is making the plan. I will trust and obey. The blessings will follow.

Trust in the Lord with all your heart and lean not on your own understanding; in all your ways acknowledge Him, and He will make your paths straight. (Prov. 3:5,6)

Ponderings

Life holds many curiosities. I find myself pondering them frequently. Call it an inquiring mind, a thirst for knowledge, scientific interest, or whatever you will—I just have questions. I'm going to share some of these perplexities with you and show you the extent of my deep thinking. Here goes:

Why would anybody want to use recycled toilet paper?

Why are ninety percent of flannel shirts plaid?

How do you shoot the breeze? You can't see it, so how could you possibly shoot it?

How do you entertain a motion? Throw it in front of a TV set with a bag of popcorn and a Coke?

Why do restaurants ask if you want a small, medium, or large drink when they give free refills?

How do you draw a blank? With an eraser?

Did Adam and Eve have belly buttons? Why would they? (I asked my grandpa, a very godly man who knew the Bible inside and out, and he responded with, "Do you?")

And lastly, where does dust come from? I personally don't know the answer to this question, but I do have a vast knowledge of the subject. You see, I'm a self-proclaimed dust expert. That's because I have so much of it.

The Bible tells us that we all came from dust, and I'm assuming it's because there was such an abundant supply available. My kitchen bears a plaque that says, "This house protected by killer dust balls." The truth is, I'm saving them up in case God needs them. The longer I keep these fine particles of matter, the more they take shape. Eventually, maybe they'll turn into a person. Admit it; wouldn't this method be a whole lot easier than going through a nine-month pregnancy and the seemingly endless drudgery of labor?

Do you know that dust is collecting on you at this very moment? It doesn't matter if you are sitting, standing, walking, or sleeping. A multitude of little, bitty, floating morsels are congregating on your body, and they are summoning their friends to party down with them. Isn't that a happy thought?

Dust likes us and our stuff. It wants to stick around. Have you noticed that after you diligently toil to obliterate the pesky parcels with a can of Pledge and a rag, they instantly reappear? The reason? Dust is everywhere and is destined to be with us forever. Another happy thought!

But, here's the good news. God is everywhere, too! Even some places dust can't go. There is no place God isn't. That's a profound statement, and I'm not really sure it's proper English, but it's true.

This gets me pondering again. If God were here in person, would we react differently in certain situations? Would our conversation at the dinner table have a little less spice? Would our road rage become a pleasant Sunday afternoon drive? Would some of the television shows we watch be left to miraculously disappear into the airwaves? How would we handle an emergency or a trauma? Would we more willingly leave hardships in His care? Would we trust more and worry less?

Just because we can't see God doesn't mean He's any less real in our lives. He is always there for us, and He's not going anywhere—ever. That's a promise, and it's a fact! Isn't that the happiest thought of all?

Where can I go from Your Spirit? Where can I flee from Your presence? If I go up to the heavens You are there; if I make my bed in the depths, You are there. If I rise on the wings of the dawn, if I settle on the far side of the sea, even there Your hand will guide me. Your right hand will hold me fast. (Ps. 139:7–10)

Now, That's Embarrassing!

Believe it or not, there have actually been a few times in my life when I've said, "Did I do that? Did I say that? Did that really happen to me?" Once or twice I've even turned a shade (or shades) of red.

There was the time I rode to a women's retreat with a vanload of highly spiritual women, including the pastor's wife. Being the big helper that I am, I gave directions to the driver. I knew we had to turn right when we got to the church named Immaculate Conception. So what did I say? "Turn right when you get to the Intimate Conception." After boisterous laughter broke out, I realized my mistake. Not knowing how to get out of this, I simply replied, "Well, most are!"

My son, Ryan, and I were shopping for a new pair of shoes. We browsed the racks at Carnival Shoes and had some good mother/son bonding. You know how moms can do two things at once? Well, as my eyes focused on the shoes in front of me, I reached my right hand backwards and groped for Ryan's. There it was. I grabbed his hand, swinging it in jubilance. The love flowed from my heart through my hand and into his. This was my son, my first-born. What a beautiful, tender moment we were sharing together. This mom stuff is great! Wait a minute, though. Did Ryan have a sudden growth spurt during our shopping excursion? *My, what big hands he has,* I thought. Glancing down, I noticed something strange. This was not the hand of my beloved young son; it was the hand of the speechless sales associate! Oops! Immediately my eyes were drawn to some interesting shoes three aisles away. Now my thoughts were, *Where is that rotten kid anyway? How dare him leave my side like that!* Needless to say, when I found Ryan we split in a hurry and found some marvelous shoes in an-other store.

As a teen, I helped with the Chapel on Wheels at the fair. During my spare time I enjoyed the exciting rides. I had befriended one of the carnival kids, and on this occa-sion he joined me on the Rock-o-Planes—my favorite. As we rode together, our legs touching, I started to get a warm and mushy feeling all over me. Was it love? No, Mr. Tough Carny Boy just lost everything he had eaten that day, and I found it—on my lap, my shoes, my socks, my shirt. How special! The child's chunky discharge sloshed around on the seat and floor of our little cage. Up and down and all around we went. When the cage turned over, the liquid dripped on us. When the cage rocked, it oozed out the door. When the ride was over, I wanted to make like a tree and leave, but I didn't have a ride home. I called my parents and waited about an hour for a change of clothes and hope for my future. Do you know what it's like to be drenched in vomit? No place to hide. No way to get away from the stench. Life doesn't get any better than this!

I became the new sideshow at the fair. As passers-by commented on my fragrance, I informed them it was a new

French perfume I was wearing—Eau de Pu. I watched people catch a whiff of the peculiar smell and then start sniffing their friends and family members next to them. They curiously scrutinized the soles of their shoes thinking they perhaps had carried away a "gift" from the stables. Bystanders, caught up in the thrill of the fair, immediately changed expressions from delight to ones of gasping for fresh air. I inconspicuously tried to shrink into the shadows. Now, that's embarrassing!

Thinking back on that day gives me an appreciation for how Jonah must have felt. He was getting the ride of his life—up and down and all around—when finally the big fish that swallowed him lost everything he had eaten and spewed Jonah forth. Jonah was one of the chunks sloshing around on the floor of the big fish's belly. Out he came, aroma putrid, looking like a freak show. His skin was white from the fish's stomach acids. He was clothed in seaweed and slime. Jonah didn't have parents nearby to call for help. He had to deal with it on his own.

Was Jonah embarrassed? I think so. His appearance was a reminder of his disobedience to God. People probably made comments and asked questions. "Jonah, what's wrong with you? Why do you look so weird?" What could Jonah tell them? "Uh, . . . this big, huge fish gobbled me up and spit me out." Yeah, right! Like people would believe that one. Jonah must have asked himself, "What if I had obeyed God in the first place? I wouldn't have to put up with this embarrassment now."

Sure, Jonah ended up doing what God wanted, but he learned a hard lesson in the meantime. Disobedience brings consequences. It's a lesson we try to teach our children. It's a lesson God tries to teach us. God disciplines us because He loves us and wants us to learn. He doesn't want us to repeat our mistakes. He doesn't want us to live in embarrassment.

I don't like embarrassing situations, especially when they are a result of my disobedience to Him. I want to obey. I don't want to give God a chance to use His creativity on my behalf like He did with Jonah. Besides, there aren't any big fish in my neighborhood. God might have to use a giant box elder bug to swallow me up and spit me out. Oooh! Imagine the nasty stain that would leave. How embarrassing!

My son, do not despise the Lord's discipline and do not resent His rebuke, because the Lord disciplines those He loves, as a father the son he delights in. (Prov. 3:11,12)

Mitad Del Mundo

W hile I lived in Quito, Ecuador, as a foreign exchange
student my loving family recorded a little jingle and sent it
to me. It went like this: "Pig guts taste better. Corncobs
taste better. Tongue tastes better. Everything's better with
Blue Bonnet on it." Actually, I had never heard the Blue
Bonnet tune before; it was new to me until I returned to the
states. But the pig guts, corncobs, and tongue, among other
unique specialties awaited my palate daily.

In Ecuador, rice and soup were served with most meals.
My first lunch there included a colorful bowl of soup that
smelled appetizing but presented a curious problem. Small
sections of corn on the cob floated in the broth along with
assorted veggies. I hadn't been trained in proper Ecuadorian soup-eating techniques, so I was in a quandary. What
do I do with the corn? I paced myself thinking I might
catch a glimpse of someone else tackling the corn issue. It
never happened. Therefore, I took a deep breath, squared
my shoulders, faced the problem confidently (almost), and
handled it my own way. I very discreetly ate the corn, cob,

and all. Yum, yum! Naturally, as soon as I finished my process, I noticed others picking up the cob, nibbling off the corn, and placing it nicely back in their bowls. Boy, did I feel stupid! If nothing else, I got my roughage for the day.

A week later, I opened the refrigerator door to find a long, pink, disgusting-looking thing with huge taste buds staring at me, only to discover it was lunch for the day. Cow tongue. I get the willies now just thinking about it.

The Ecuadorian eating excursion continued. I ate goat, soup with pig guts, as well as many other foods new to a sixteen-year-old foreigner. To top off the trip, on my last weekend there I "enjoyed" one of the country's delicacies— guinea pig. Do you know how hard it is to feed on something with its beady baby blues glaring right at you and its four legs sticking straight up in the air? Especially when at home the little fur ball would be merrily running around in a cage, bringing great joy to all the kids in the household? Being the thoughtful teenage daughter that I was, I returned home with the remains of my tantalizing treat carefully tucked away in my travel bags. I wanted my parents to know I was thinking of them.

Don't get me wrong. Ecuador has many wonderful foods that are hard to beat. For example—bananas. Nothing compares to bananas ripened on the tree. The taste is out of this world. There are several types of bananas, too, which was news to me. Bananas for eating raw, bananas for frying into chips, and bananas for baking (a sensational dessert). They are all luscious. The coffee and cocoa grown in Ecuador are unmatched. And then there was a special kind of bread, *pan de agua*, that did my heart good. I loved it! I still find that occasionally my mouth and tummy yearn for the taste of Ecuador.

Being a *gringa* in a foreign school brought a challenge or two. During the first week of classes, one of my teachers had the nerve to ask me if I had a problem understanding the material or if I was "slow." I s-l-o-w-l-y explained to her that no, I wasn't slow; I just had a problem with the language. Through all this, I wondered if my teacher was "slow," because I was the only blonde, fair-skinned girl in a class of very tan, dark-haired students. Plus my name, Twila, is not your typical Ecuadorian name. In fact, they don't even have a "W" in their alphabet! Oh, well.

My first name did bring some confusion, though, and was hard to pronounce. However, my last name, Francisco, fit right in. There are lots of Franciscos in Ecuador, but usually it is a first name. A nickname frequently used for Francisco is "Pancho" or "Paco." I became "Paquita," an endearing term for Paca (female for Paco). My name change was certainly easier for my friends and acquaintances to handle and I felt more comfortable in my new surroundings.

I had the privilege of becoming friends with the Ecuadorian president's daughter. Actually, she was a very close friend of my Ecuadorian "sister" and I got to tag along with them periodically. I even had the opportunity to visit the presidential palace. Aren't I hotsy-totsy?

On the flip side, to add a little twist, another of my "sisters" was married to the son of a man who tried to overthrow the government during my stay. A short war broke out and opened my teenage eyes to another world. The sound of gunshots penetrated my bedroom. Airplanes blasted through the clouds outside my window. For a while, my "sister" and "brother-in-law" took refuge in the basement apartment of our house because of kidnapping threats. Later we went by the presidential palace and noticed the bullet holes and broken windows. My Ecuadorian family was in a unique situation. They had interests on both sides of the war. Talk about exciting!

Another two-sided thrill for me was the day we journeyed to *Mitad del Mundo*—middle of the world. I have an unforgettable memory of standing on both sides of the world, the equator between my straddled legs, my left foot in the Northern Hemisphere, and my right foot in the Southern Hemisphere. That was an experience that doesn't happen every day in the physical sense.

When the time came to leave Quito I cried and cried. I had become friends with my new world and grew more comfortable every day. I delighted in my life there. But I was an Iowan, and it was time for me to cross the equator and return home to my real family. That world and those experiences are behind me now. I haven't returned and probably never will, though my life is left with a lasting impression.

The book of Genesis paints a picture of Abraham and Lot standing at a point where they could see two lands. Abe gave his nephew the option of living wherever he wanted. Lot's eyes and senses were drawn to the lush plain of the Jordan. The distant towns called out to him. He yearned for the sights, sounds, smells, and tastes of the city. The idea of "the good life" was planted in his mind and started to take root. Lot chose to stake his tent near Sodom and live among the cities of the plain. He didn't think about his future. His decision was made to satisfy his immediate worldly desires. In time, Lot became too comfortable with his surroundings and gradually was sucked in by the enticement of evil. Lot made his abode in Sodom, the sphere of sinfulness. Lot and his family conformed to the world.

Lot's choice of worlds made a lasting impression on his life. I'm sure he never forgot the family and friends he lost in the destruction of Sodom and Gomorrah. Every time he salted his food, he had a vivid reminder of the wife he no longer had.

Meanwhile, Abraham moved his tents throughout Canaan, staking his claim to the Promised Land. He had a close-knit relationship with his Heavenly Father and was transformed continually by the renewing of his mind. Abe strove to do God's will and lived in obedience to God's commands. He was a witness to those around him but did not take part in their lifestyle. Abraham lived in the realm of righteousness. His citizenship was in heaven.

In a spiritual sense, we have two worlds fighting for our allegiance. One world, which tries to move our focus off the Lord and His love for us, is continuously trying to overthrow our desire for being in the Father's will and obeying His commands. As Christians whose citizenship is in heaven, we need to cross the spiritual equator from the sinful sphere to the righteous realm. We must not become too comfortable with the wrong surroundings and wrong ideas or we will too easily be sucked in. We must choose the world in which we live. We cannot straddle the line and stake our claim on both sides. There is no middle ground. No compromise.

What is before you? Are you following Jesus? Are you friends with the world or friends with God? Some of the words of a familiar hymn say, "I have decided to follow Jesus. The cross before me. The world behind me. No turning back. No turning back."

The world and its desires pass away, but the man who does the will of God lives forever. (1 John 2:17)

A New Heart

It was an unusual March night. Steve and I actually got out of the house without Ryan and Laney, then three and a half years and twenty-two months old. We even had a real baby-sitter, someone other than Grandma. We wrote down the phone numbers of the places we'd be and headed out the door with our friends. Yippee! This was too good to be true. Or was it?

My bowling shoes were on my feet and I was ready to give the pins a little action, when over the loudspeaker I heard, "Twila Belk, please come to the counter for a phone call." It was Marie, our baby-sitter. "Your mom just called. Your dad went into a coma on the bathroom floor. They are on the way to the hospital now." Shock. This was totally unexpected. My dad was extremely healthy, still playing softball at age 58. We rushed home, made arrangements with Marie, and had our night out—at the hospital.

About Dad—he was silly, creative, and maybe a tad crazy. He had a goofy response for almost anything. Tell him you had a headache—"Stick your head through a window and the pane will be gone." "Where's Mom?" "She broke her leg, and we had to shoot her." Something really nifty? "That's slicker than snot on a doorknob!" If it was super slick, it was a glass doorknob. When following a woman who had a bit too much wiggle in her waddle—"It must be jelly, jam doesn't shake like that." Heading out the door, saying your good-byes—"See you in the funnies!" Or, if you were bold enough to say, "See you later!" he might answer with, "Thanks for the warning." The tradition continues as Steve and I have inherited many of his expressions.

Dad was a jokester, too. He purchased a life-like rubber hand and one day got the notion to close it in the trunk of his car, with the fingers sticking out. Reactions from other drivers were varied. Some didn't know what to think. Many found it hilarious—except for the policeman who followed Dad home to question him.

Our pastor's jaw was broken when he used it to catch a speeding softball. His mouth was wired shut for some time, allowing him to speak only in a garbled, mumbled fashion. My dad stood up in front of the congregation at church one Sunday and announced that he had a special message from Pastor Johnson. What was it? "Mmmph, mmmph, mmmph."

I remember when Dad helped serve ice cream for a church social. He was feeling a little feisty when he dished up a bowl for our pastor's son. Instead of ice cream, Paul received a heaping helping of leftover mashed potatoes, drizzled in chocolate syrup. Yum, yum!

When Steve and I were dating and he came over for his first family meal, he got a surprise. Dad knew his nickname was "Rabbit," so while we said grace, a Bugs Bunny style carrot was deposited on Steve's plate. Throughout the years, Steve discovered at mealtimes that Dad was good at depositing his corncobs, chicken bones, and other nonedibles on Steve's plate, too. I guess it was Dad's way of showing that Steve was part of the family.

Popcorn and ice cream were two of Dad's favorite foods. (After a bit of arm twisting, Steve took it upon himself to carry on the Francisco heritage.) Dad freely shared these foods with his little white dog, Muffy. The dog Dad had wanted nothing to do with when we first brought her home was now eating from his spoon. Muffy quickly became Dad's best friend. She slept curled up in his arm after giving him a lick bath each night. Any time she heard Dad's keys jingle, she darted out the door and hopped in the car to join him for a ride. Whenever Dad was out of town for days at a time, Muffy grieved, but she instantly perked up the minute he returned. They had a special relationship.

Dad was a very giving person. He'd give the shirt off his back if needed or even the car he was driving, for that matter. He gave of himself constantly to help others, asking nothing in return. Dad was brilliant—a self-taught lawyer. He assisted people with legal problems and helped farmers who were losing farms due to foreclosure. Helping and giving his time to others was the essence of who he was.

Dad was, and always will be, my hero. He stood up for what he believed in, no matter the cost; and there were occasions when his beliefs cost him big time. Everything he did was for the benefit of other people: his grandchildren, his family, and his friends.

Now, back to the story. Doctors said Dad's brain was hemorrhaging—an aneurysm. Stubborn Dad had been hit with a severe headache earlier that day, making his legs wobbly and too weak to stand. He asked Mom to take him to a chiropractor, thinking an adjustment would help. Later that evening he collapsed on the floor, responding to nothing. Muffy paced back and forth by his side, guarding him, licking him, ready to bite anyone coming near. She sensed that something was seriously wrong.

Dad was in a coma for five days. I kept vigil at the hospital day and night. We were allowed to see him only periodically, and I didn't want to miss one opportunity to be with him. We looked for a grasp of the hand, a fluttering of the eyelid, a response in recognition—anything to give us a glimmer of hope. Finally one evening, after keeping constant watch on the machines connected to him, the doctor informed our family that Dad would be brain dead by morning. A group of physicians consulted with us and asked if we might consider organ donation. They explained how lives were saved using other people's organs. Dad's situation made him a perfect candidate for this process. Knowing that giving was Dad's nature, we agreed to offer whatever he had.

A strange and interesting aside here: when Muffy went outside to do her business that day, she crossed the road—something she never did. Muffy was hit by a car and died simultaneously with her best friend.

After tests detected no brain activity, Dad was pronounced dead, but his body was kept functioning through life support. A team of doctors from Iowa City came in to surgically remove his organs. We were told that Dad's fifty-eight-year-old heart was as strong as that of a twenty-year-old. Meanwhile, a fifty-eight-year-old man desperately in need of a new heart and compatible with my dad's was located. He was flown to the University of Iowa Hospital, ecstatically anticipating his new life. At that time, my dad's heart was the oldest heart yet used for a transplant in the United States.

Knowing that Dad's heart gave someone life brought great joy to Mom. She wanted to know as much as possible about the recipient, but due to hospital regulations details weren't allowed to be released. Through a series of unusual circumstances, we discovered the man's name and the town where he lived. Mom contacted his wife and before long became acquainted with this special man—even meeting with him face to face a few times.

Mom's new friend shared the story of how he was close to death, barely able to breathe. His heart was functioning like that of a ninety-year-old man. The doctors told Lawrence that his only salvation would be a new heart. A phone call at midnight brought him the good news. The voice on the other end explained that they had a heart donor. A hospital airplane transported Lawrence and his wife to Iowa City, getting them there by two A.M. He claimed he was so excited he could have flown on his own power. While the hospital staff prepared Lawrence for surgery, my dad's heart arrived at four A.M. At 6:30, they did the transplant, and finished surgery by nine A.M. How miraculous! Within a matter of hours, a dying man was given hope for his future. Part of my dad was still alive, offering new life for a joy-filled person. To see Lawrence strong and healthy did wonders for Mom.

Mom and Dad had no health insurance, no savings, and very little life insurance. Dad's doctor bills and hospital bills accumulated to huge amounts. Steve went with Mom to explain the situation, to plead mercy, and to make payment arrangements. When Mom received the next hospital bill, she broke down in tears. The balance read zero. The entire debt had been written off. Talk about grace!

Oh, what a beautiful picture the Lord gave me as I thought about Dad's story. I caught a glimpse of Christ on the cross, His arms stretched out, willingly dying so that we might live. The only thing that can save us is a new heart—His heart. As our hearts, dying in sin, are yielded to Him, the Master Physician transplants His heart into our bodies. He lives in us! We are given a healthy new life, filled with future hope. He offers complete grace and mercy as our debt of sin is canceled. Balance zero. Paid in full. Unspeakable joy is ours for the asking.

Thank you, Jesus. And Dad, see you in the funnies!

I will give you a new heart and put a new spirit in you; I will remove from you your heart of stone and give you a heart of flesh. And I will put My Spirit in you and move you to follow My decrees and be careful to keep My laws. (Ezek. 36:26,27)

The Big Announcement

It was the big day, the day I'd drop the bomb. I was nervous and excited as we neared the part of our church service when we shared praises and prayer requests. After a couple of people spoke I raised my hand. My turn. I stood up, and through my mouth flowed the words that had been rolling around in my head over the past month or two.

"Last year, when we closed StraightWay, it was a very difficult time for us. Shortly after closing, a wise woman of God gave me a word from the Lord. She said that we were there to fill a gap, and now God had something bigger and better for me to do. Naturally, I've wanted to know what that bigger and better thing was. Since that time I've been asked to do many important things, but God made it clear to me that no, I wasn't to do them. One thing I thought I'd do is write a book, and I still plan on doing that someday. Another idea I had was this: I've been working out and lifting weights since January, and I've lost about fifty pounds. I thought, wow, if I kept at it and got myself biffed up, I could be kinda like Arnold Schwarzenegger and go around the world in my bikini lifting weights for Jesus. Or, maybe I could start a female version of the Power Team. Then I thought maybe I could go around singing opera and give people's ears a thrill. After all, I bought myself one of those special hats with the horns and braids. But, for some reason, God did not give me the go ahead on either of those ideas. So I said, 'Lord, whatever You have for me to do, I'm willing.' Well, you have to be careful when you tell God 'whatever.' You can get into a lot of trouble that way. God is full of surprises, and I'm living proof that He has a sense of humor. So, it is with joy and great amazement I'd like to announce that on or near my thirty-eighth birthday in early February, I will be giving birth to the next Billy Graham." (Yes, I really did say all that in church!)

At this point jaws dropped and people went into a state of disbelief. All kinds of shocked reactions followed. It was so much fun! They didn't know where I was going with my little speech. Some figured it out before I finished, but Pastor, among others, was tongue-tied. I loved every minute of it.

The incredible thing to me, though, was that three pews in front of me sat my doctor. Rita and her family just happened to be visiting our church that particular Sunday morning. When I was about halfway through my announcement, she started to crack up. She knew what was coming next and almost made me get off track. What were the chances of her being there the day I chose to let the world know? (By the way, she hasn't forgotten it. She mentions it every time I go in for a check up.)

After the initial feelings of wonderment began to sink in, the congregation demanded a response from Steve. He stood up and declared, "I'm forty!" The look on his face was priceless. Needless to say, our church service wasn't quite the same after all that, but there was a sense of merriment and joy in the air. This has given me something to chuckle about for a long time.

Now, let's backtrack a little bit. Summer vacation was here and I felt wiped out. Why was I so tired all the time? I was beyond functioning. Vacation Bible school was over and that had been a big responsibility because I was the director. Maybe that wore me out. We had been having loads of company. Maybe that was it. Ball games almost everyday. I was too pooped to poop. I got nothing done around the house and I wanted to nap constantly. Eventually I started to notice other changes. Normally I loved coffee, but now I couldn't stomach it. I began to get queasy on and off.

No, it certainly can't be. Impossible. I've been off birth control for over ten years and nothing's happened. My body is goofed up. I can't get pregnant. Hmmmm, better rethink that. It's amazing what removing a major source of stress will do, along with exercise and losing weight.

During one of Ryan's baseball games, when I was all alone, I sneaked into a store and inconspicuously purchased one of those nifty little tests. I kept it hidden, fearing someone would notice. Steve was at Promise Keepers and Laney was at camp. Later that night, after Ryan started snoozing soundly, I tiptoed into my bathroom to begin the testing process. With timidity and trepidation I opened the box, did my duty, and waited. Time's up! I checked it. *Maybe it needs more time*, I thought. I looked again after awhile. *Could be I'm just reading it wrong.* Afraid not. "You are pregnant" was the message trying to seep beneath the thick outer layer of my brain. The message wasn't getting through. Shock. Denial. Disbelief.

Steve, when told of my secret, was ecstatic. He was thrilled with the idea of being a daddy again. It had long been a desire of his heart. Oh, I've got to admit that I was a little excited, too, but I couldn't help thinking how old I was. *I can't remember how to do this. It's been too long. The baby will just be starting kindergarten the year Ryan graduates. I'm ready to retire. What will people think?* And lastly, *How did this happen anyway?* Duh, Twila.

I felt somewhat like Sarah who laughed hilariously when told she was pregnant. Yes, Isaac was the first name we considered. I empathized with young Mary, too. I know she experienced some of the same feelings I did when Gabriel let her in on God's plan. The shock, the disbelief, the embarrassment, the "what will people think" syndrome. But Mary was available to do whatever God wanted. She was God's servant, and the rumblings of the relatives or John Q. Public didn't matter to her. She had a very special job to do, and God had hand-selected her to do it.

Because of my surprise pregnancy, we have a precious little man named Jesse—a blessing to family and friends. Because of Mary's surprise pregnancy, we have the Savior of the world—a blessing to all mankind.

Blessed are you among women, and blessed is the child you will bear! (Luke 1:42)

The Rude Intruders

Bug n 1: a nasty, little, creepy-crawly insect that irritates the living daylights out of you 2: not a welcome guest, but an unwelcome pest 3: a rude intruder

Box elder bugs. They are everywhere and they are disgusting. I don't know if your part of the country has ever seen them, but where I live in Iowa (at least at my house and every house we've ever owned) they are more prolific than flies on garbage. Rumor has it that they are somehow associated with box elder trees, a type of maple tree grown here.

I'm befuddled when trying to figure out why God, in His infinite wisdom, created them. I've been told that animals won't eat them because they are bitter to the taste. (I guess we won't be dipping any in chocolate for a savory sweet!) And poor pet lizards can't even digest the bugs because they emit some kind of poison repulsive to the reptiles. So why, why, why has God graced my place with truckload upon truckload of these pesky little varmints?

One day it hit me. I pictured God in a deep voice saying, "Twila, I gave you these bugs as an illustration of sin. You, in turn, must take what you've learned and educate the multitudes." Yes, God is right. The traits of these insects and the characteristics of sin are parallel in many ways.

So, multitudes, are you ready for the lessons I've gained and the life applications I've received from God's invasion army? First, I will introduce you to the brazen behavior of the box elder bugs. Here goes—

Box elder bugs congregate in huge clusters on the outside walls of our house and garage. They saunter here and there, hanging out behind the shutters, under the shingles, on the window ledge, or wherever their teeny legs will take them. On warm sun-shiny days, it'll appear as if parts of our house are black and moving because of their huge numbers. It's almost as if the sunshine exposes the bugs' secret sanctuaries and they are drawn into the light.

The bugs especially like to linger on windows and doors. Their conspiring minds realize these entrances will eventually open up a whole new world for them to inhabit. Sometimes a few will slowly creep into our home through an inconspicuous hole or crack. But, look out! When we open the door, they flock inside like there's no tomorrow. Some of the lazier ones will jump on our shoulders or land on our heads for a free ride in. They're not dumb. If they have someone willing to carry them, they'll go for it!

Immediately the box elder bugs set up camp, and nothing is considered off limits. They hang glide from wall to wall, bungee jump from the chandelier, catapult off the curtains, and hold quilting bees in the corners. They march their holiday parades on the ceilings, become the table runner at meal times, and oversee the daily dishwashing operations. We find them doing the backstroke in our lovely beverages, and their playgrounds are our plates of food.

Another major annoyance of our constant companions is the "special" red poop spots left behind on our freshly painted walls, curtains, and paperwork. My sister-in-law Ruth informs me that box elder bugs don't poop, they spit up. Whatever this nasty habit is called, I don't like it.

After a while, we get accustomed to having the bugs around. We casually overlook them or pretend they aren't there. I tend to become fairly comfortable with them and start giving them names. This allows us to chat on a more personal level. Sometimes visiting friends who aren't acquainted with our houseguests appear alarmed when greeted by them. I'll simply introduce them by saying, "This is Herman. This is Fred. This is George. They're part of the family."

I've noticed that Fred, Herman, and George like to travel. On several occasions, I have arrived at my destination, opened my purse, and watched in amazement as they traipse out. I'd exclaim, "Guys, what are you doing here?" and they'd inform me that they had recently joined the visitation committee. How embarrassing!

I remember sitting at Bible study one Thursday morning when my leg began to itch. Reaching down to scratch it, I felt a strange bump and decided to investigate. Lo and behold, Herman was trapped there between my skin and pantyhose – and still alive! (This gave new meaning to the expression "my skin is crawling.") I must admit that this was a little too intimate for me. I didn't know how to react, so I opted for laughter rather than screaming. Besides, I had a great time of show and tell after Bible study.

Removing these pests is not always an easy project. If one lands on me or near me, I'll haphazardly flick it across the room with my thumb and middle finger. This does nothing but causes others to get in line for a ride. What do they think this is, an amusement park? I've found you can't be easy going with these creatures. You have to take drastic measures to eliminate them!

At first, people claimed the only way to destroy box elder bugs was to dowse them with hot, soapy water. Yes, this worked, and they were also very clean when they drew their last breath, but you can't exactly dump hot water on your walls and furniture. This is an outdoor technique.

Another extreme means of execution is to squish them. When I smash them, I'll usually announce, "He won't have the guts to do that again." (It's an important part of the process!)

My favorite death trap is what I call "box elder bug hell." Whenever the halogen lamp in our living room is glowing the bugs are enticed by its light. They crawl over to check it out and are fried to a crackly crunch before they know what hit them. This is very effective, but the resulting stench is horrendous.

After many years of mixing potions, the pest control companies have finally created a formula that will extinguish these insects. But just when you think you've got them licked and they've disappeared for a while, they'll start to pop up again. You must be on constant guard.

"How does sin compare to these unwelcome visitors?" you ask. Well, sin, like these bugs, hangs around waiting to find a way into our lives. Sometimes a few little sins will sneak in through an opening we didn't know existed. Other times sin will see an unguarded door and think it's an invited guest. Often, it's encouraged to come in, even offered a ride. Sin doesn't miss one opportunity to come and live with us. It is a rude intruder.

Once sin enters our lives, it sets up camp. It spreads out into every corner of our hearts and minds and takes control of our routine business. It affects all areas of our existence. We become sin's playground.

Sin leaves its mark on our lives. There are consequences that must be paid as a result of sin, and many times we are left with permanent stains or nasty reminders stemming from our wrong actions and choices.

Eventually we feel pretty comfortable with sin. We get used to having it around or we even casually overlook it. Our friends or other people, when accosted by it, see it for what it is—sin. At that point we, too, need to accept it as sin and not try to cleverly disguise it as "my friend, George." We must give sin names like jealousy, bitterness, anger, resentment, self-centeredness, or gossip, and deal with it.

Our bitterness, anger, and jealousy like to travel with us, too. In fact, they go everywhere we do and end up adversely affecting our relationships with others.

When Christ's "Sonshine" floods our life, sin is brought to the surface and its hiding place is exposed. Sin cannot endure the Light.

In order to get rid of sin we must take drastic measures. We can't just nonchalantly flick it back and forth. We must stamp it out.

God's formula for sin control is to acknowledge it, confess it in Jesus' name, and repent; then the blood of Jesus Christ will cleanse the sin from us (just like the hot soapy water treatment). If we don't take this step, we'll end up like the crispy critter in the halogen lamp—burnt! We must be constantly on guard, because when we don't deal with sin daily, it rears its ugly head again.

Reading 2 Samuel 11 and 12 reminded me of King David, who at one time had a bug infestation problem. It started out innocently enough; he just didn't go to war when he was supposed to. This left the door open for a bitty bug called "lust" to enter in. This little bug had such a great time setting up camp that he invited some of his other buddies to join him. One by one, this invasion army marched into David's life and eventually took over. Some of these pests were adultery, lying, attempts to cover up wrongs, and murder. The more bugs David let in, the more they grew in clusters.

King David was feeling pretty comfortable with his bugs. He tried to casually dismiss them with words or other poor choices instead of exterminating them permanently. This led to more and more problems for David, affecting many people and many relationships. These bugs left some terrible stains on David's life—his child born out of adultery died, he had to live knowing he had killed an innocent man, and other consequences resulted as well.

Thanks to a prophet named Nathan, who shed some light on David's pest problem, the bugs came to the surface and David realized he had sinned against the Lord. He pled for forgiveness and for the hot soapy water treatment—that his bugs of sin would be washed away and cleansed. He confessed his guilt and prayed for pardon and restoration. David's sin involved others, but he recognized that it was primarily against God.

Yes, King David at times had bug problems, but he knew the correct steps to take to rid himself of this pesky population. God was able to use David in mighty ways.

Hopefully, we can learn a lesson here. Let's extinguish our bugs before they become a major annoyance. We can call up God's pest control service and wash those rude intruders away!

Box elder bugs are God's creatures put on earth to give us heightened awareness of sin. Sin is Satan's work and will bug us constantly. What's bugging you, a bug called Herman or a bug called Sin?

If we confess our sins, He is faithful and just and will forgive us of our sins and purify us from all unrighteousness. (1 John 1:9)

Mud Bath

Ever notice how kids and mud go together like peanut butter and jelly? Mud is magnetic; kids are drawn to it. And it doesn't matter how old they are, either. Give them an acre of kid-friendly grass to play in and they'll find the one mud puddle tucked out of sight. It's inevitable. A favorite expression of parents over the years has been, "Stay out of the mud!"

There is a creek down the hill from our house, and our kids love to go there with friends. The creek forms a pool with deeper water in one spot, creating a fun place to play. Sometimes they'll take bait (cheese slices, corn, hot dogs, or bologna) and fish. Other times on hot, boring days, the kids will invariably ask if they can swim in the creek. I shudder when I think of the critters lurking beneath the water waiting to permanently attach themselves to unsuspecting skin. On the other hand, I don't want the kids to miss out on any important childhood memories. Therefore, being a pushover mom, I allow the adventure, but not without sending a saltshaker to season any leaches attempting to eat my child for supper. I also insist the kids wear their grimiest clothes.

After an hour or two, I'll hear kids' voices and notice soggy bodies sloshing up the hill. More often than not, they are drenched with gooey glop oozing from their pores. Sand and slime are embedded in their scalps and clothing. It's not enough that the creek water is filthy, they can't resist the temptation to sling and smear mud, so they have a mud fight—and a good one at that. When their feet hit the deck outside the dining room door, I say, "Stop right there and strip. You're not coming in the house like that." Dirty duds are discarded all over the deck, and the kids tiptoe to the nearest shower to clean up. As the sun dries their clothes, they become so stiff they stand on their own. The clothes can't be worn again, but they make fantastic Frisbees!

During our youth leader years, Steve and I planned some wild and crazy parties. One particular party we dubbed "Almost Anything Goes." We did some wacky things like throwing bucket loads of water balloons off the church roof to see how much water the kids could catch and save. We played water balloon volleyball. In the parking lot, we slung watermelons from a sheet to see how far the seeds would splat. We tossed raw eggs back and forth. All kinds of bizarre games. But the most memorable were those done at the mud hole.

We dug a deep hole in a big open area and filled it with water. Stretched across this pit was a large PVC pipe on sawhorses. The object of the game was to scooch all the way across the pipe carrying a nine-inch rubber ball. Sounds easy enough, but there was a catch—the pipe had been greased with Crisco. This added a little excitement. One by one, brave souls slowly progressed, ball in hand or under shirt, clinging as best they could to the slippery pipe. Many didn't get very far before surrendering to the mud hole. Others got further but eventually became suspended upside down above the pit, appearing amazingly similar to a sloth. They hung on for dear life until finally doing a full layout Tsukahara into the muck below. Very few reached the finish line mud free.

Because we wanted to provide an equal opportunity for all wannabe wallowers, our next game included everyone in the slime pit at the same time. Marbles were strewn throughout the mud hole. The contest was to see which team could retrieve the most marbles in a given amount of time. Grappling and groping in the thigh-high goop for several minutes gave the kids first-hand experience of a pig's life. Of course, we slopped "the hogs" with some yummy food later in the day, but not until they were well hosed down first. What a mess, but what fun!

As much as big kids like playing in the mud, little ones love it more. There's just something special about splashing in a puddle or sliding head first across the grass during a downpour. Always, after getting good and grimy, they present themselves at the front door, smelling like something that died. Pheweee! Time for a bath.

Mom or Dad plops the piglet into the tub and carefully but thoroughly begins the scrub-down. Behind the ears, around the neck, between the wiggling toes, under the grungy fingernails—every crack and crevice, every nook and cranny, is soaped, washed, and rinsed. Squeals of delight erupt as water is splashed up and down and all around, so much that all involved in the process are soaked. When the filthy bath water is drained, the no-longer-piglet reaches up with tiny arms and a trusting smile. A large, fluffy towel with a heavenly spring-fresh scent is wrapped tightly around, but not as tightly as Mom's or Dad's hugs. As the terrycloth dries the bitty body, the wee one is caressed, sung over, loved, and tickled until gleeful giggles burst forth.

The grubby garb is done away with, and clean clothes or jammies are slipped on over sweet smelling skin. There is nothing quite so soft, squishy, and delightful as a freshly bathed child. Don't you just love it?

This tender care reminds me of the way Jesus treats us when we decide to put our faith in Him. He pulls us out of the slimy mud hole of sin and says, "No more of the pig's life for you. From now on you're a sheep, and I'm your Shepherd. You'll find that hanging out in pleasant pastures beats wallowing any day." Then He says, "Pheweee! It's time for a bath!" and proceeds to cleanse our every nook and cranny, crack and crevice with the blood that He so lovingly shed at Calvary. No more mud—we're clean at last. Jesus gently picks us up, enveloping us in His larger-than-life arms. He tells us that He loves us more than words can express and that He's thrilled we now belong to Him. As Jesus snuggles with us, we have an overwhelming sense that to Him there is nothing so soft, squishy, and delightful as a freshly bathed child. (Me!) Then we remember that our grimy garments were thrown away—we have nothing to wear. Before we even finish that thought, Jesus takes off the robe He is wearing and slides it over our shoulders. He wraps it tightly around us and we breathe deeply of the lingering heavenly scent. Righteousness radiates from our new attire. We feel fresh and squeaky-clean. The smell of death is gone.

Glancing in the mirror, we notice a distinct difference in our appearance. It's amazing how much we resemble Jesus while we're wearing His clothes. As Jesus meets our eyes in the mirror He says, "You're all cleaned up now. You can go out and play carefully, but remember to behave like a King's kid. And, one more thing—stay out of the mud!"

I delight greatly in the Lord; my soul rejoices in my God. For He has clothed me with garments of salvation and arrayed me in a robe of righteousness. . . . (Isa. 62:10)

Orphaned

Let's see—there's do-si-do, promenade your partner, and, of course, allemande left, allemande right, stand up, sit down, fight, fight, fight! I had to hone up on my square-dancing terminology. After all, I hadn't square danced since grade school.

The beautiful early October evening and the country home made the perfect setting for the barn party our friends were throwing. Everyone from church was invited. My family was energized. I knew this square dance would be an experience we'd never forget. Later we realized how true that statement actually was.

Mom's house was on the way to the little town of Argo, so we picked her up en route. I insisted she join us, even though she wouldn't dance, because she needed the fellowship. Our son Ryan spent the night with a friend, but six-year-old Laney was prepared to party.

As we unloaded from the van at hoedown headquarters Mom smiled and had a twinkle in her eye. She wore a teal blue T-shirt my sister-in-law gave her for her last birthday.

It stated, "I'm not 60. I'm just 18 with 42 years' experience." The shirt and Mom's glow were a winning combination. "Am I being a little too bold wearing this shirt here? People might think I'm looking!" She laughed. I chuckled with her and reminded her she could only wear it one more week. Mom beamed and seemed to look forward to her night out.

That night we square danced ourselves silly. We promenaded when we were supposed to allemande. We do-si-doed when we were supposed to promenade. We forgot which foot was our left and which was our right. But even with our confusion, we had magnificent fun with old friends and new. Mom got a kick out of watching the sometimes indistinguishable dancing and spent the time chatting with others while sitting on a bale of hay.

Because we didn't want Mom to get antsy or bored, we left a little earlier than the rest of the crowd. As we headed toward her home, we recapped the evening's enjoyment. That's all I remember.

I was groggy. My eyes fought to open. I kept hearing voices. "Twila! Twila!" Ridiculous questions like, "How much do you weigh? What day is it? What is your name?" Excruciating pain.

I opened my eyes again. White uniforms frantically scurried around me. Voices tried to hold my attention. *What is this hard thing I'm lying on? Why am I in such pain? Where am I? I can't be here. I have lunchroom duty at school next week. I have to play the piano at BSF. Oh, the pain!*

Again my eyes fluttered open. There was my brother Gary, holding a big mug of coffee. *His eyes sure are glassy!* There was Lynn, my sister-in-law, and Jennifer and Nancy, my dearest friends. *Boy, do I hurt! Can I get some medicine? This too shall pass. It's only temporary. I can make it.* I continued to submit to drowsiness.

During my in-and-out state of consciousness, I learned we had been in a terrible accident. Hit by a drunk driver. Laney was upstairs in pediatrics with Nancy and Jennifer watching over her. I was in the emergency room. "What about Stephen? What about Mom? Are they okay?" I was repeatedly assured that everyone was fine. Steve and Mom were at the other hospital in town.

As a large crowd gathered around me I was handed the phone. "It's Steve," they said, "calling from his hospital room." He was sobbing uncontrollably. "I'm sorry, honey. I'm so sorry. Your mom didn't make it. They wouldn't let anyone tell you. I couldn't stand it anymore. I had to call. I'm so sorry."

"That's okay, honey. It'll be fine." I was tired; my aching body was in shock. The magnitude of this information could not fully register with me at the time. I needed to heal first before it could sink in.

I was bleeding internally. My body had been crushed. My situation was touch-and-go for a while, and the doctors didn't know if I would even make it. The communication lines to heaven were kept very busy as people all over the country prayed on my behalf. God intervened and changed the course my body was taking. I would be fine, but it would take up to six months to get my full strength back. (There's no reason I should be alive today, but God wasn't finished with me yet. I still had work to do.)

During my ten-day stay in the hospital, bits and pieces of information filtered in. Our accident was a very news-worthy event. Something relating to it was on the television news or in the paper every day for a week. Jerry, the twenty-eight-year-old man who caused the fatal wreck, had been drinking in two taverns. His blood-alcohol level was almost three times the legal limit. Ten minutes before our crash he had been involved in a hit-and-run. His drinking buddy, riding in the passenger seat, was so fearful he jumped out of the car a short time before our accident. We also learned that Jerry had previously been arrested three times for drunken driving and he didn't have a driver's license or insurance.

Because of the grace of God, my husband and I were able to forgive Jerry instantly. People didn't quite under-stand, but who are we to say we're better than God by not being able to forgive? If God can forgive us so freely, then surely we, as His children, must be willing to do likewise. Later, a very traumatic trial process brought us face to face. Jerry's eyes were dark—filled with hatred, anger, and bit-terness. There was no repentance. No remorse. He main-tained throughout the trial that we were to blame. For some reason God filled me with compassion for his lost soul. I wept when he was sentenced. I continue to pray for his salvation and look forward to the day I learn he's a brother in Christ.

My mom's funeral took place while I was in the hospi-tal, the day before her sixty-first birthday. There was no closure for me. After a few months of healing, reality hit. At age thirty-three, I was an orphan. My best friend, part-ner in craziness, my right hand, helper, the one I could count on for anything, the one who comforted me, coun-seled me, stood up for me, was gone, never to return. Life would be different, but I would have to keep on living.

I can imagine this is how the disciples felt when Jesus told them He would be leaving. Their friend, their partner, the One they counted on for everything, was going to leave them. He was going to die. "But, I won't leave you here by yourselves. I'm sending Someone just like Me to take My place." This "Someone" would continually be with them in the form of the Holy Spirit—counselor, helper, comforter, advocate, and friend. Life would be different for them, and they would have to keep living, but now they'd have the help and strength they needed with them at all times, internally instead of externally.

This internal strength and comfort is there for all of us who believe. Jesus did not leave the disciples or us abandoned. What an embracing thought!

I will not leave you as orphans; I will come to you. (John 14:18)

Surprise!

I love the element of surprise—when it's coming from my direction. Dropping in on people to help them celebrate an important event when they least suspect it is great fun. So is the offering of unexpected gifts.

When my oldest brother, Marvin, turned forty, we thought it would be a fantastic idea to pop in and see him; it would be only a nine- or ten-hour trip to his home in Kansas. My husband and I, my mom, and our young son and daughter carefully and enthusiastically planned our agenda. We painstakingly strategized every minute detail for this exciting expedition. We were in cahoots with my sister-in-law, Virginia, who was preparing the particulars on that end. This was going to be too good.

With Virginia's assistance, the staff of the K–12 school where Marvin was principal arranged for a big student assembly in the auditorium—complete with entertainment and black cupcakes. A large appliance box would be on the platform, festively decorated in birthday wrap. The plan: my brother would be encouraged to "open" the box and receive his reward tucked inside—Mom. The rest of us would then trot on stage. It was a perfectly devised scheme—surprising not only my brother, but also his two children who attended the school. We could barely endure the wait to carry out this conspiracy.

Finally the day of our adventure came. For a timely arrival we traveled halfway the day before, staying in a motel overnight. We left the motel the next morning at the precise moment gauged to reach my brother's house at noon, where Virginia would be waiting for us. My husband, Mom, and I were wild with excitement—the butterflies doing back flips in our bellies.

Twelve o'clock on the dot we pulled into the driveway. Mom jokingly asked, "Wouldn't it be something if Marvin were home?" As if on cue, my brother walked out the front door. *The creep!* The surprise was on us! Naturally, we all had questions. Why was he home? He never comes home for lunch. (He used the lame excuse that there was a grass fire nearby, and he felt he should check on things for safety's sake.) *Why did there have to be a grass fire on this particular day?*

When Marvin showed up at home, my sister-in-law panicked. He wanted to know why she wasn't at work. She suddenly feigned an illness. She wanted to know what he was doing and why, meanwhile secretly praying that he would be gone before we appeared on the scene. No such luck. The timing was perfect—for him! *The creep!* We were stuck in a terrible predicament and had no choice but to tell all. In my loving, sisterly way, I let him know that I was not pleased.

Well, it was decided we still needed to execute the plan, despite the fact that my brother was aware of every detail. We would become actors. He would act as if he were surprised and unsuspecting. I would act as if I didn't want to kill him. It was a hard thing to do – acting civil and pleasant to my brother's associates while clenching my teeth and grumbling at him under my breath. We did it, though, and the students were thrilled to participate in this "shock" for their principal. One good thing happened—my niece and nephew were caught unaware and delighted in the celebration.

Today we laugh about it, although it's several years later and my blood still boils just thinking how he foiled our flawlessly engineered affair. I don't know if I'll ever let him forget it. *The creep!*

Surprising my second oldest brother, Mel, wasn't as bad, but he had me worried for a while. For his fortieth birthday, my family hopped an airplane and flew to Texas. (It was my children's first plane ride—exciting for all of us!) My brother and family from Kansas drove in for the occasion, too. We met at my uncle's house, along with our grandpa and Mel's daughters.

Mel and my sister-in-law, Char, were spending the weekend at a hotel in town and had arranged to enjoy a nice birthday dinner with our aunt and uncle. When arriving at our uncle's, they walked into the living room and engaged in stimulating conversation. We sauntered in from our secret stations to surprise him. His reaction: "Oh, I see you made it here okay." Thank goodness, that was his shock speaking, because it almost sounded as if he were expecting us. Eventually the reality of it all sank in. He was amazed and thrilled that we went out of our way to share this special time with him.

For Char's fortieth a few months later, I sent ice cream. Now, don't be thinking I've gone off the deep end. This isn't your ordinary ice cream—it's Whitey's ice cream—the best in the Midwest and quite possibly the whole world! (Whitey's originated in our area and is one thing my brother's family has missed since moving away.) I ordered enough malts for Char, Mel, and their three daughters; Whitey's packed them in dry ice, FedExed the treats to Texas, and they were enjoying them within forty-eight hours. This was definitely a sweet surprise that was savored and talked about for months. A little extravagant, but worth every penny because of the great impact and lasting memories it caused. I could hardly wait for the phone call I knew would be coming in response.

Surprises sure can be fun, can't they?

I've noticed that God loves the element of surprise, too —even more than I do. Right from the beginning of time, God pulled off one surprise after another.

Imagine Adam's astonishment when he woke from his God-induced nap to find a curvaceous, two-legged creature with long, flowing hair nearby. I believe his exact words were (although they can't be found in the Bible)—"Whoa, man! What is this I see, standing next to me?" (Not only was he the first man, but the first poet as well.) To this day, her name is woman, a shortened version of Adam's immediate expression.

Can you picture Noah's wonderment when he looked out of the ark and saw rain for the first time ever? Did he say, "Wow! God's never done it this way before!"? I'm certain Noah was overjoyed knowing he had been obedient. God *did* keep His promise after surprising him with such a strange and lengthy work order.

How about Pharaoh's overwhelming feelings of amazement when plague after plague attacked the nation of Egypt? Blood. Frogs. Gnats. Flies. Disease. Boils. Hail. Locusts. Darkness. Death. Did he wonder, "What kind of God is this that has so many tricks up His sleeve?" Then the shock of the Red Sea opening to let the Israelites cross, only to close and gobble up any pursuing Egyptians. Leave it to God to have such creative ideas.

God really did a number on a sweet little Jewish girl named Mary. He stunned her with the news that she would bear the Christ child. I can almost hear her now, "Joseph, *Joseph*! We've *got* to talk!" What a surprise, but what a blessing and honor to have such an important appointment.

The Bible is full of unexpected occurrences, but my favorite is the most momentous and significant—the now-you-see-Me-now-you-don't event, otherwise known as Christ's resurrection. Jesus came back to life after suffering a horrible crucifixion. Men and women were startled, bewildered, perplexed, flabbergasted—words that don't do justice to the scenario. Never before in history, and never again, has anyone beaten the power of death. No other god can make that claim. Jesus Christ is the One, true, living God. Because He rose again, we have a future hope. We can overcome our obstacles. We can be victorious.

Now that's a surprise with a lasting impact!

Why do you look for the living among the dead? He is not here; He has risen! (Luke 24:5b–6a)

Weirdin' Out

I was in a state of disbelief. My jaw dropped in profound amazement. My eyes blankly stared in wonder. I asked, "How can this be? Why would people lose all control of their body, mind, and spirit like this?"

It was obvious that a very powerful force had caused what once were considered sane people to go stark raving mad. Symptoms of their condition included irrational and obsessive behavior, maniacal tendencies, and unreasonable and senseless conduct, all very similar to a person possessed. In other words—they were weirdin' out.

"What was the cause?" you ask. Believe it or not, a hunk of cloth sewn around some beans and fluff stuff, with a heart-shaped tag attached for effect, otherwise known as Beanie Babies. Teenie Beanie Babies to be exact.

I'm referring to a time when the McDonald's fast food chain had a Teenie Beanie Baby promotion. Do you remember it? They offered twelve different critters in this highly collectible series. The special toy was received with a Happy

Meal or could be purchased separately if a food item was bought with each one. Someone told me there were enough of these Teenie Beanies manufactured for every person in the United States. (Not that every person would get one, of course.)

There are many stories to tell about the strange she-nanigans of the human animal during the first few days of this beanbag craze. Frenzied people furiously flocked to and packed McDonald's restaurants all over the area. The fire marshal shut down one particular site locally because it was crowded to over capacity.

Men and women came with their strategically laid out battle plans. Friends and relatives stationed themselves at various locations alerting each other via cell phone or pager when their particular restaurant released the next Beanie. People stood in line for hours with expectations of getting the entire series. Grandmas and grandpas worked out deals with people in front of them in line. Grown adults made outrageous demands. Pushing. Shoving. Bad attitudes. Not a pretty sight!

A guy in the parking lot sold accessories that collectors supposedly can't live without: tag protectors and display cases. By mid-afternoon of the second day of the promotion, his stock of 4,000 clear plastic boxes was gone. Crazy!

People arrived in the drive-through at 12:30 A.M., choosing to spend the night so they would have first dibs on the "treasures" when the hamburger joint opened. Others circled the drive-through every hour in hopes that a different prize would be available. One woman pushed her dune buggy around and around so it wouldn't overheat as she stayed in line all day. Not my idea of a productive day!

Traffic piled up for blocks causing near accidents and traffic jams, because a woman refused to pull forward in the drive-through lane until the next Beanie was offered. She would not budge. The manager insisted she move. She would not budge. The manager called the police, who asked her to move. She would not budge. The police called a tow truck. She budged!

Our poor, clueless friend, Gary, made the mistake of stopping at McDonald's for breakfast with his nephew on the way to Sunday school. He had a hankerin' for pancakes and had this absurd idea that he might be able to enjoy some at his favorite fast food place. He was in shock when he couldn't get in the door. After trying another location with the same results, he settled for stale donuts from a gas station. Imagine that. A guy couldn't even buy himself breakfast! What is the world coming to?

Speaking of Sunday school, some regular attendees skipped in order to stand with an unruly mob and collect their toys at McDonald's. Seems to me there's something wrong with this picture. Then there are the people who don't go to church at all because they don't have time for it, yet they can stand in line at a fast food restaurant for an entire day, maybe even overnight.

I decided, with tongue in cheek, that a great marketing campaign for the church would be to offer Beanie Babies to all those present on Sunday mornings. People would come in throngs, and for once we would have standing-room-only crowds. There would be three available in the series:

♥ The Beanie Preacher—Preachers are already referred to as men of the cloth, and some of them are full of beans and fluff anyway! (Pastor, duck, or you'll get beaned with a left jab!)

♥ The Beanie Bible—A way to get a Bible into some homes or a way to get others to pay attention to it. How about a deluxe version for the coffee table?

♥ The Beanie Cross—Maybe a way to make people realize the significance of what Christ did for us. If the message were written on that heart-shaped tag, it might sink in and be treasured.

People could come to church for their "Happy Meal." They could feast on the Bread of Life and quench their thirst with the Living Water. Unlike McDonald's, there is no charge for this "Happy Meal" or the prize received with it. The love of Jesus is free, and there is enough for every person in the world.

Do not store up for yourselves treasures on earth, where moth and rust destroy, and where thieves break in and steal. But store up for yourselves treasures in heaven, where moth and rust do not destroy, and where thieves do not break in and steal. For where your treasure is, there your heart will be also. (Matt. 6:19–21)

Lessons from a Sixteen-Month-Old

Toddlers are certainly a truckload of fun, aren't they? Observing our little man Jesse as he approached toddlerhood gave me plenty to think about. I contemplated some of the great miracles in the Bible and how they would be different if they involved a sixteen-month-old. The first one that came to mind was the walls of Jericho.

For six days the armed men marched around the city. On the seventh day they marched around Jericho seven times. The priests blew the trumpets, the people gave a loud shout, and the walls came tumbling down. I am convinced that having a toddler available would have saved Joshua's men tons of time and effort. There would be no need for marching, no need for trumpets. Just one of the child's practice-makes-perfect, ear-piercing, shrill screams, and the walls would be shattered in no time flat. Then Joshua would stand up and in his commanding voice ask, "Was that real, or was that Memorex?"

Another option for David, rather than stoning Goliath, would have been to leave a shoe laying around. The toddler would saunter over, pick it up, and wallop the giant on the forehead at close range. (With the heel, of course!) Before the giant knew what hit him, he'd be down and dirty with a headache the size of King Kong. If a shoe wasn't handy, the sixteen-month-old could be plopped in his highchair and left to pelt the giant with peas. After a couple minutes of this bombarding, Mr. Goliath would be running home to Mama.

Remember the stories of famine and drought in the Bible? If they had turned a teething toddler loose on the dry fields, the never-ending faucet of drool would have irrigated the crops in a hurry.

How about when Jesus fed the 5,000 with just a few loaves and fishes? I found that happening at my house every day. After giving my little man his baby-sized portions, he miraculously multiplied it, and I picked up twelve baskets full off the floor from each meal.

In case you were wondering, I write of these new and unimproved miracles from personal experience. Also, I have an increased awareness of how Sarah must have felt raising a baby at her age—*very old*! How did she keep up with Isaac? All I know is that Sarah must have been an incredible woman. Maybe she just kept laughing all through Isaac's childhood. That would have kept her young.

As I watched my toddler live his young life day after day, I thought of all I could learn. He taught me about my relationship with God. In God's eyes I'm just like little Jesse is to me; I'm learning about God's world and growing as His child.

When a baby first learns to walk, he teeters around, sometimes taking a step or two, sometimes bonking his head. After consistent practice, he gets the hang of it and walking becomes natural to him. In our Christian walk, we start out taking baby steps. It's all new. There's so much to learn. At times, we stumble and fall, but God our Father gently picks us up and lovingly sets us on the path again.

It's a process that gets easier and more natural with time. And for our benefit, God in His wisdom gave us a manual on how to walk—His Word, the Bible.

Curiosity aroused my little tike. He raced around the house with his index finger in the air, spontaneously pointing and exclaiming, "Dat! Dat!" He was discovering new things in his world. He also liked to open every door and drawer in his way, remove all objects from any surface up to tippy-toe height, drag everything imaginable from the pantry into the living room, and unfold each basketful of freshly done laundry. And that was just in the first five minutes of his day! Sometimes the things Jesse did were accepted and sometimes they were not. Mom or Dad let him know in a hurry if it was a no-no. We also taught him what "hot" meant and what his other potential danger zones are.

We grownups are curious, too, and sometimes we like to test the waters with God. God tries to teach us which things are too hot to handle or what will hurt us. He gives us boundaries and rules for a purpose. If we cross over the line, the result is discipline. He loves us and cares about what happens to us. He does what He can to steer us away from danger zones as we operate in our free will.

When the time came to return the crib we had borrowed (our friends Gary and Lorraine had a "surprise" come along, too), every naptime and bedtime thereafter became a long, drawn-out ordeal. We put Jesse in bed. He crawled out. We put him in bed again. He crawled out again. Over and over. Just like a yo-yo. Little did Jesse realize that Mom and Dad knew when he should be in bed, and it sure would have been a lot easier if he had just obeyed and stayed there. How often are we like that with God? He tells us to do something, and we try to crawl out of it. Over and over. Yo-yo obedience. When will we learn that it's easier and a lot less tiring if we obey God the first time?

There were times little Jesse would cry and reach his tiny arms up to us to receive needed comfort. No one can soothe away the pains of life quite like Mommy or Daddy. Other times something would excite him, and he'd squeal with delight, bringing great joy to our parent hearts. It's comforting to know that our Heavenly Father is always there as we reach up to Him in tears. He calms us and carries us through our trying circumstances. He's thrilled when we respond to His blessings in joy and loves to hear us sing praises to Him.

My favorite part of parenting Jesse when he was smaller was when he climbed into my lap and melted into my arms. He snuggled in, nuzzling his precious face next to mine. Immediately his third and fourth fingers went into his mouth, and he started sucking contentedly. I wanted to squish him and squeeze him and eat him up; I just couldn't help myself. I felt like I couldn't get enough. To me, that was pure luxury. Imagine how the Lord feels when we climb up on His lap and want to nuzzle and cuddle with Him. He can't get enough! He's waiting for us with strong, wide-open arms, full of love and hugs. When we spend time with Him in the Word, worshiping Him, praising Him, and conversing with Him, we are in a sense melting into His arms, giving Him the devotion He deserves. To Him it's pure luxury. After all, that's why we were created!

I'll be the first to admit that parenting doesn't always come easy. At times, I get so frustrated and exasperated that I feel like pulling out every hair on my head and chinny-chin-chin. My impatience causes me to wonder why God ever wanted me to have kids. But then I look at the sweet, innocent, puppy-dog look in my child's eyes, and I realize how I've been blessed beyond measure. One morning, as I watched Jesse in his highchair, I reflected on what a cherished gift he is and had a rush of love flow through me. God reminded me through my toddler how treasured I am to Him.

Jesse. God exists.
How could anyone think differently after seeing you?
The softness of your hair, your eyes, and your skin all speak of God's gentleness to us.
Your precious smile reminds us of how God smiled down on us—especially when He created you.
Your sweet voice, like the sweetness of God's Spirit, bringing unspeakable joy to our lives.

You sit in your highchair,
smashed bananas smeared on your face,
rice cereal plastered in your hair.
You are special.
You are unique.
Set apart to do God's work even before you were born.

Thank You, Lord, for entrusting us
with this outpouring of Your love.
Help us to be faithful to Your call.
Guide us as he patterns his steps after ours.
It's a big job, Lord, knowing that we are raising up
a servant of the Most High God.
Give us strength and courage to do what is right.
Help us to seek Your face continuously.
He's Yours, Lord.
Make him into a man after Your own heart.

How great is the love the Father has lavished on us, that we should be called children of God! (John 3:1a)

I Yam What I Yam

I'm Popeye the Sailor Man,
I'm Popeye the Sailor Man.
I'm strong to the "Finich"
'cause I eats me spinach.
I'm Popeye the Sailor Man!

Popeye. I yam what I yam. When I was a kid, Popeye was one of my favorite cartoons. He inspired me. Here was a weak, scrawny, wimp of a man who could do anything with the overwhelming power of spinach. He'd get in a pickle with Bluto, the big brute, or need to rescue Olive Oyl when she was in a pinch. When stuck in a corner or in tight spots, Popeye didn't panic. He chug-a-lugged a can of spinach and became an instant strong man. He tackled any predicaments in his way. Popeye was pitiful in his own strength, but could do mighty things with great power when he took advantage of his glorified greens.

Thinking back to my childhood days, I can't help but wonder if this cartoon was a giant marketing ploy paid for by the spinach companies. I know it caught my attention. I was convinced this vegetable was the answer to my problems. I was determined to be like Popeye and insisted that I be allowed to eat a can of spinach.

My mom gave me some coins and let me walk to the small grocery store next door. (Was she laughing under her breath knowing what was to come?) I returned with my prize purchase, anticipating the surge of strength that would explode through my body when I downed the miracle meal. "Twila, it tastes really good with mayonnaise on it. Why don't you try it that way?" I always trusted my mom's advice and thought, why not? As the bowl was prepared, I rubbed my hands together in excitement. I had the key to continuous power at my fingertips. My life would never be the same.

The first forkful of high expectations went into my mouth, the flavor rapidly reaching my taste buds. Interesting. Oooh . . . *Yuck! Ptooey! Gag!* The spinach immediately did a U-turn and sped the opposite way. It didn't stop to ask directions. It got out of there and in a hurry. That was a nasty trick! And my mom was so quick to go along with my plan. I thought she loved me! (Now, if Popeye had used Popsicles, things would be different.)

Because of this little episode, I was leery of trying spinach ever again. When I was dating Steve his mom cooked some one night and they were enjoying it together. "It's good with vinegar on it," they declared. Being a brave soul, I attempted to taste it. Oooh . . . *Yuck! Ptooey! Gag!* No, thanks, I've had enough.

In recent years, I've found that fresh spinach is the way to go. There's nothing like a good spinach salad or some crisp spinach on a sandwich to add color and taste. Spinach dip is very appetizing, too. However, I'm still a wimp and a weakling after indulging myself with Popeye's claim to fame.

In the Old Testament there are many accounts of wimpy people accomplishing great and mighty things. How did they do it? They had the power of One who called Himself, "I Am Who I Am."

Joshua had the jitters. He was just one man who was supposed to lead a vast multitude into the Promised Land. There would be many obstacles along the way—nations to overtake, people problems to deal with, rivers to cross, big decisions to make. How could he do it all? Over and over we see the Lord saying, "Be strong and courageous. Don't be terrified. I'm going before you and will always be with you. My power can do the trick." And it did.

Samson, at his weakest moment, blind and reduced to humiliating slave labor, was brought out to entertain the Philistines as they praised Dagon, their fish-head god. Did he juggle, do cartwheels, and dance? I don't know, but he put on such a great performance, he brought down the house—literally. The temple where this grand celebration happened was crowded with men, women, and all the Philistine rulers. At least 3,000 people were on the roof, too, watching, mocking, and sneering as Samson was made their sport.

Well, Samson had endured enough of these shenanigans. He cried out to the great I Am Who I Am, pushed on the pillars, and—*crash! boom!* They all fall down. With God's power working through him, he accomplished more in his puniness than when he was a strong man. Take that, you fish head!

We all know about David, the pipsqueak of a kid who tackled lions and bears and eventually the mammoth man, Goliath—the one who caused all the Israelite warriors and their macho king to shake in their boots. David repeatedly said in the Scriptures, "It is God who arms me with strength." Wow!

After Jesus died and was resurrected there was a power shift. The same power available externally to our heroes in the Old Testament now became available internally to all believers—the power of the living Christ in the form of the Holy Spirit.

Paul, in the New Testament, bragged about his weaknesses because they prove to us how powerful God is. Check this out—he worked harder than anyone else, he was imprisoned more frequently, flogged more severely, exposed to death again and again, five times he received forty lashes minus one, three times beaten with rods, stoned once, shipwrecked three times, spent a night and day in the open sea, was constantly on the move, faced danger from this, that, and the other thing regularly, etc. Now, wouldn't that make you a weak piece? I think yes.

But Paul said he delighted in weaknesses. He delighted in insults. He delighted in hardships. He delighted in persecutions. He delighted in difficulties. Why? "For when I am weak, then I am strong." Is he nuts? No. He just knows what God can do through weak pieces. Paul took a lickin' and kept on tickin'. His difficulties challenged him to draw on God's supernatural power, and, except for Christ, he accomplished more for the kingdom than any other man.

Guess what? We have difficulties. We have it rough sometimes. But the power of God within us is greater than the troubles surrounding us. When we grow weak in our struggles, God's strength will prevail—not our own.

Popeye took advantage of the power spinach gave him. We must learn to take advantage of God's power. How? By being weak. No problem!

I feel a song coming on—

I'm Twila the Lord's woman.
I'm Twila the Lord's woman.
I finish so strongly
'cuz I have the power of the living Christ within me.
I'm Twila the Lord's woman!

Hmmm—doesn't quite flow, does it?

But by the grace of God I am what I am, and His grace to me was not without effect. (1 Cor. 15:10a)

Gotta Tell Somebody!

Do you ever get a feeling deep down inside you, a feeling that if you keep it in you're gonna erupt? If you don't get it out, you'll explode? I do. And I'm not talking gas bubbles here. Sometimes I get so filled up with joy it seems like I'll burst. I just gotta tell somebody!

One thing I know is this—God is good. All the time! He loves to indulge us, to show us that He cares. Everyday He sends hugs and kisses, His blessings, little reminders of His great love. Are we paying attention? Do we see Him in the little things? Can we see His hand of provision? His sense of timing? His faithfulness?

I firmly believe that the more our eyes are opened to God's fingerprints, the more faith we have. When we notice the little things He does for us on a regular basis, the more we can trust Him for the big things. When we see Him working in our lives in good times and bad, we get all excited and want to tell everybody. When we tell others, they are inspired to walk forward in trust and hope. You can't lose when you keep your eyes fixed on God.

I gotta tell you some of the things I've seen or experienced God do over the years. Some may seem small, and others nearly took my feet along with the socks when they were blown off, but they all point to an awesome, loving God.

One day I told a friend how I'd been praying for my son to do well at baseball tryouts and for him to get on the right team. He said, "God doesn't care about stuff like that." It was all I could do to keep myself from going into a three-hour rendition of what I will call "Oh, how wrong you are, Bucko!" God cares about every little detail of our lives, including baseball. And, believe it or not, underwear. Yes, underwear. I remember a particular day when I had run out of all my lady Fruit of the Looms. I hadn't washed clothes in ages. To me this was a problem. I prayed, "Lord, You know how much I like to wear underwear. Please have some miraculously appear so I can happily cover my rear." The Lord humored me and, after digging through my dresser drawers for the umpteenth time, I found a pair peeking out between the piles. God cares about underwear!

A couple of winters ago, on a frigid Iowa day, I needed to get some things at Sam's and Wal-Mart. I had no choice but to take baby Jesse with me. I didn't know how I could carry my little man bundled in his snowsuit, my purse, and my purchases while keeping Jesse's face covered from the below zero wind. I asked the Lord to give me a parking place right between the two stores, next to the shopping cart corral; that way I could manage Jesse and my purchases conveniently. I was very specific with my prayer. In faith I drove down that aisle in the parking lot knowing God would grant my request. You know what? Ever since then I automatically drive to that spot, and there is always a nearby place for me. Pretty cool, huh? God cares about parking places!

Our kids had been hounding us for a dog. We put them off for as long as possible. We were leery, especially after having had a bad experience with Spiker, the "dog from hell." God knew we needed the right dog, and we asked Him to make the choice clear to us. We met Max, "the wonder dog," at the Humane Society and put him on hold until we could purchase the needed doggy supplies. We checked prices at several stores and returned to Sam's for the doghouse. After loading the igloo style home on a flatbed along with a bag of Puppy Chow, we headed toward the checkout counter. A man and woman approached us from who knows where and blurted out, "This is kind of a funny thing to say, but lost our dog, and we have a doghouse just like that we would give you." Okay. I guess that could be interpreted as a sign that Max, the wonder dog, was God's choice for us. We followed these godsends to their home a few blocks away and left with a wonderful doghouse, a couple of doggy dishes, and confirmation that Max was meant for us. To be at Sam's at just the right time and the right place, and to have these people waiting there for us was all divine intervention. God saved us big bucks and reminded our whole family of His love. God cares about dogs!

My daughter Laney's desire for a couple of years was for a certain type of coat. There were many particulars she wanted – the style, the pockets, the right football team (Chicago Bears), etc. She needed a new coat, but I knew what she wanted came at a higher price than I cared to pay. I tried to talk her out of it and into something less pricey. One catch, though. Her brother had one, why couldn't she? "Okay, Lord, You know the situation here. Show me what to do." I looked in a sporting goods store thinking that if any place had the coat they would. The store had plenty of coats, but not Laney's team. High prices, too. I decided to check out another store before returning home, figuring they definitely wouldn't have it. When I got there, I noticed only four or five coats hanging on a circular rack. On closer examination, they had one Chicago Bears coat, size medium. Hey, that might work! I checked the price. Above the rack was a sign, "40–60% off." With my five-dollar coupon, the coat was cheaper there than at any other store, and at a price I would gladly pay. We lovingly referred to my prize purchase as "the miracle coat." Laney knew it was a gift from God. God cares about coats!

My mom always made an angel food cake for my birthday. When she died God tapped my dear friend Jennifer on the shoulder and put her in charge of this little detail. She has carried on the tradition every year. One time I had unexpected guests for supper and didn't think there would be enough food. When I opened the box of taco shells, there were extras inside. I prayed for a Christmas poinsettia during one of our financially lean years, and my husband received one as a gift from a Sunday school student. Isn't God good? Just knowing He cares about seemingly insignificant details like these means the world to me. Nothing is too small for God's attention.

God does big things, too. After closing our Christian bookstore a few years ago, we had lots of leftover product sitting around—boxes of cards, music, gifts, books, office supplies, video cases, and a bunch of little piddly odds and ends. We also had an overgrown sales counter, a Bible imprint machine, pieces of slatwall, shelving, hardware for hanging things, and various do-dads. We had stuff stored in the garage, in bedrooms, in the basement, and in the breezeway. It was coming out our ears! What could we do with it? It was valuable, too good to throw away, but of no use to anyone without a store. So we lived with it, secretly wishing it would magically disappear. Eight months after we closed StraightWay we got a phone call from another Christian store in the area. They were planning to open a second store in a different town and wanted to know if we had anything left. Oh boy, did we ever! They took everything we had, including the space-taking sales counter. We were paid on the spot. What a glorious day! It was during this time that we were experiencing some heavy financial distress and didn't know how we would pay our bills. Only God could have orchestrated something so thoroughly.

After my dad died, I saw God's hand of provision for my mom continually. Not having insurance and working only part time, Mom had many bills. We saw God wipe out many thousands of dollars worth of hospital and doctor bills. Whenever Mom needed money, it was there. One time she found a thousand dollars under her bedroom rug. I have no idea what caused Mom to look under the rug, but I'm sure glad she did. Many times when bills came due, she didn't know how she'd pay them; but after getting the day's mail, the money would always be there for her. Her purse was stolen from our bookstore one Christmas Eve day as she helped us. She was devastated because she had just been to the bank. At church that evening, she was presented with a monetary gift that more than covered her loss. Her roof was badly in need of replacement. There was no way she could afford it. God sent hail, the insurance company inspected the roof, and Mom got a new roof absolutely free. What a blessing to see God work.

I have experienced God's intervention in my life when I was near death. Recently the perfect job fell into my lap, when I wasn't even looking. Money has fallen from heaven right when my family needed it. Nothing is too big for God to accomplish.

A vanload of friends and I were on a trip to the Mall of America, six hours away. It didn't occur to any of us to check the gas level until we were almost there. The tank was empty; we were riding on fumes. Within a few seconds, we came to a gas station. It was the last station in sight before we got to our destination. God's timing was perfect.

Another situation when God's perfect timing was at work was when we purchased our current home. Our friends had seen the "for sale" sign in the yard one January morning on their way to church. Knowing the house was in the area we wanted, they told us immediately. We checked it out, fell in love with it, and put in an offer right away. Our offer was accepted; we just needed to sell our house. Month after month went by and our house hadn't sold. Meanwhile, realtors busily showed our "dream house" to prospective buyers. I was on edge. God knew that this house had everything we'd ever wanted. It was even on the right road. Why were we being tempted with the perfect house when someone else would probably get it before us? Finally, our house sold, and we moved in mid June. But, in the interim, the septic field had been tested and found to be faulty, costing thousands of dollars to be replaced. In January, when we placed the offer, the ground was frozen and the septic field couldn't be checked. With the delay, we ended up with a brand new septic field and weren't burdened with the headaches this caused. God had all the details figured out beforehand.

God's timing was evident one summer when our son became critically ill. My grandpa died, so Steve, Laney, Jesse, and I traveled to Kansas for the funeral. We left Ryan, our eldest, at home with a friend to play in a baseball tournament. During our absence, Ryan's appendix ruptured. His high pain tolerance enabled him to endure what he thought was the flu. Once we returned home, we realized his serious condition. In less than an hour, we were en route to the emergency room and Ryan underwent an emergency appendectomy. He was barely able to withstand the twenty minute trip to the hospital. If Ryan had traveled with us to Kansas, we wouldn't have been able to bring him home; he was in too much pain. Both he and Steve had wanted to go on a missions trip to build houses in Mexico with our youth group, but all the positions were filled. Ryan's appendix ruptured here while the youth group was in Mexico. If he had gone on that trip, he might still be in Mexico. The timing was such that Ryan missed only a few tournament games and ended his baseball season on a high note. God's timing is always perfect.

Why am I telling you all this stuff? To uplift your hope. To remind you that God cares. To encourage your faith. To increase your awareness of God's presence in your life. I've learned that because God cares about the little things and the big things, because His timing is always perfect, because He is always faithful, I can trust Him with everything. So can you.

Did God do something neat for you today? Did something silly happen that brought you joy? Did He bring special people into your life right when you needed them? Is God working, blowing your socks off? Then tell somebody! Testify to the awesomeness of God.

They will tell of the power of Your awesome works, and I will proclaim Your great deeds. (Ps. 145:6)

Ointments

Question of the day: What do you put on a burnt pig? *Oink*ment! I can't help but think of that silly joke every time I hear the word "ointment."

When Oreo, our poor kitty, was covered with fleas, my husband returned from the nearby vet's office with packages of ointment. We needed to apply this product under her coat of fur at the back of her head. Magically, the fleas died within twenty-four hours. I was surprised by the concept of flea ointment and marveled at the vast array of ointments on the market. In fact, most homes have several varieties lining their shelves.

An item I periodically used as a new mom again was diaper rash ointment. Some types are white and creamy, clearly noticeable when smoothed on the little one's behind. Others are greasier in nature, allowing the baby's byproducts to slide off with ease. But both serve the purpose of alleviating a red, irritated bottom.

When our bicycling children scrape their knees or come home from creek stomping with a fishhook imbedded in a finger, Neosporin or Bacitracin is our salve of choice. First, we gently and lovingly clean the wound, and then nurse Mama's caring kiss must precede the medicine and Band-Aid. Miraculously, the owies heal within a few days when handled with this tender treatment.

The weather can't make up its mind. It's sweltering and sunny one day, frigid and snowing the next. Croupy coughs settle in. At times like these we reach for the jar of Vick's VapoRub. Massage it into the sick one's chest, turn on a vaporizer, and—voila!—the creeping crud soon disappears.

Have sore, aching muscles? Ben Gay or Tiger Balm might be the answer for you. Not only does it ease the pain, but the penetrating smell clears your sinuses as well.

Udder balm isn't only for Bossy the cow anymore. This lotion offers soothing relief for dry, cracked . . . uh . . . hands. It makes our hurting skin as smooth as a baby's (or cow's) bottom. Udderly amazing!

Everyone has a jar of Vaseline sitting around. What is it used for? Who knows? But it brings great comfort simply by being readily available.

Even vehicles need the renewing help of special ointments. We lube the joints with grease, pack the roller bearings with big globs of goo, and pour oil into the engines. All of these are essential to the high performance of our automobiles.

A soothing restorative agent not found on the shelves in the house or garage but very attainable to everyone is the Lord Jesus Christ. He is always on call. His healing balm offers unparalleled benefits. If His ointment were bottled, the label would read:

> **Directions:** For internal use only. Apply as needed to provide refreshing relief from broken hearts, burdened lives, disappointments, and loneliness. Also helpful for

calming fears and anxieties, replenishing rest when weary, and nourishing disheartened souls.

Warning: When used in its concentrated form, a joyous life might result. No expiration date.

What a great friend we have in Jesus! He cares enough about us to soothe our sufferings and heal our pains. Experience His tried-and-true remedy today!

Come to Me, all you who are weary and burdened, and I will give you rest. (Matt. 11:28)

An Interview with the Virtuous Woman
(based on Proverbs)

T B: Thanks for taking the time to sit and chat with me. It's quite an honor talking with you up close and personal like this. Your cover story in *Solomon's Digest* is the rave. You are the subject of countless books and the hot topic during bridal showers. Every year on Mother's Day your name seems to slip into the sermon. Across the nation your picture is plastered in homes of women aspiring to be just like you. I've always admired you, but I just can't figure you out.

VW: Oh, really? Why's that?

TB: You are a successful woman who is highly praised and honored. You ooze personal dignity and worth, and you are bubbling with life. You seem so perfect, so far out of reach, so, so . . .

VW: Proverbial?

TB: That's it! In fact, I don't even know what to call you. I've heard you called the Proverbial Woman,

143

the Virtuous Woman, the P31 Woman, the woman who puts us all to shame. You know.

VW: Most of my friends call me Grace.

TB: How appropriate! Grace it is then.

TB: Grace, do you mind if I ask you a few questions?

VW: It would be my pleasure.

TB: I see that your husband thinks the world of you. He has full confidence in you—even praises you in public. I've been told that you are, in a sense, the "wind beneath his wings." You enhance his standing—build him up. Tell me the truth. Doesn't he ever just drive you crazy?

VW: He has been instrumental in the development of my patience. For example, he forgets to take his sandals off at the door and sometimes leaves a trail of tunics and sashes throughout the house. Quite frequently he doesn't finish one building project before starting another. I couldn't begin to count the times he has misplaced his phylactery.

TB: How do you handle those situations?

VW: Believe me, I'm tempted to grumble, but the thought of him preferring to live on the corner of a roof or in a desert rather than with me changes my mind in a hurry. I've trained myself to remember his good qualities—how he helps with the servants or runs to the market for me when I'm sewing. It's getting to the point where he can pick out quality wool and flax for me if I need it. He works hard to give our family a good name. I have found that if I overlook his offenses, hold my tongue, and respond to him patiently and lovingly with kind and gentle words, he tends to appreciate me more. It's amazing! When treated this way, he feels like he can go out and conquer the world. I'm proud when I see the respect given him at the city gate. I love him!

TB: It's apparent from what I've witnessed that your method works. Maybe I should give it a try. What's the deal about your kids, though, bragging about you, calling you blessed, and all that stuff? Sounds pretty unrealistic to me.

VW: Respect, love, and the proper tone of voice do miracles.

TB: Ouch! That one hurt. *May the words of my mouth and the tone of my voice be acceptable in Your sight, oh Lord.*

VW: Amen.

TB: Obviously, Grace, you are in top physical condition. You rise before the rooster crows, ready to work vigorously with eager hands. You have boundless energy and strong arms to perform your tasks. How do you manage that? Do you work out somewhere? I'm tired all the time.

VW: I agree with David's tried-and-true philosophy. He said, "It is the Lord who arms me with strength." In my experience I don't get much done in my own power, but when I give control to the Lord, it's incredible what I accomplish. Because the strength is from Him, I can work with happy hands and a joyful attitude.

TB: I've noticed you make good use of your time; you plan ahead and are very productive. You are never idle. You certainly don't ever appear to rest. Do you?

VW: Over the years I've watched a lot of sluggards. I applied a lesson from my observations: "A little sleep, a little slumber, a little folding of the hands to rest—

and poverty will come on you like a bandit and scarcity like an armed man." So I've learned to plan ahead and be wise with my time. I do rest, though, but I rest in the Lord. I use my free moments to dig into the Word and pray instead of watching the camel races or involving myself in the local gossip about who is best at carrying the most water home from the local well and other non-productive, time-consuming activities. I get renewed and refreshed while achieving things of eternal value.

TB: In your hard work and planning ahead you also seem to make wise investments. It appears one of your favorite investments is people. You open your arms to the poor and extend your hands to the needy. Don't you have enough going on already without taking on this additional burden?

VW: Oh, but it gives me great joy. Every time I help someone, I am blessed in return. Solomon was right when he said, "A generous man will prosper; he who refreshes others will himself be refreshed." You should experience the delight.

TB: That is definitely an interesting concept.

TB: Reportedly, you are quite the seamstress, with one of your specialties being quilts and bedspreads. I keep watching the K-Mart white sale ads for a line of bed coverings tagged as yours. After all, Martha Stewart has hers. I was really disappointed, too, when I checked with the local merchants and didn't find your label on any of the linen garments or sashes. I would love to market your entire inventory! I'm sure there would be high demand for all your merchandise. That's something I could do, you know, since I was born to sell. I can see it now: scarlet skirts and scarves, purple pantsuits, proverbial panty liners, virtuous vests, noble nighties. And a big sign over the department: Garments by Grace—Clothe yourself with strength and dignity. Eat your heart out, Kathy Lee!

VW: Twila, that's very flattering and all, but there's one point I'd like to clear up. It's not the clothing that gives the strength and dignity; it's the lifestyle.

TB: I'm sorry, Grace. I got a bit carried away in the heat of excitement. I suppose part of strength and dignity comes from being self-controlled, too. Doesn't it? Grace, your actions and speech exude wisdom. At the beginning of your story we are told that you are worth far more than rubies. In Proverbs 8:11 I read that wisdom is more precious than rubies. Your name and wisdom are practically synonymous. After talking with you I see that. How can I attain that kind of wisdom?

VW: Wisdom is a process that stems from a right relationship with God. He gives wisdom generously to all who ask Him for it. I ask Him with every decision I make.

TB: If I am correct, much of the advice and instruction you've given me comes right from the book of Proverbs.

VW: Oy veh! That's why I'm called the Proverbial Woman!

TB: Now I'm beginning to understand. I'm going to keep studying God's Word and applying it to my life. Maybe someday I can be just like you. You have given me great hope. Thanks, Grace! Oh, and one last thing. Do you mind if I ask you something that's been gnawing at me for years? Have you ever had a problem with chin hairs?

VW: I think I must go plant my vineyard now!

The fear of the Lord is the beginning of wisdom, and knowledge of the Holy One is understanding. (Prov. 9:10)

Trash or Treasure?

You've heard the expression "one person's trash is another person's treasure." That certainly held true for a ladies' gathering we had at church. "A crazy-lady auction" the event was dubbed, and I had the honor of being the auctioneer. (I wonder if my being loquacious had anything to do with this.)

The concept of the auction was this: the ladies were encouraged to bring a few unwanted items they had sitting around the house that might be valued by someone else. To reword it—we got to bring our unused junk for some eager customer to "buy." Each woman was given the same amount of crazy-lady money to hold in her hot little hands and spend as desired. The assorted stuff—some very useful and some downright unusual—beckoned browsers to the display table. The women were all bubbling in anticipation of the treasures they hoped to carry home.

The slick auctioneer (me) tried to creatively sell people on the idea of purchasing used patterns, old craft magazines, a "lovely" green and yellow plastic canvas needle-pointed

note holder, and other rare treasures. But the bidding became heated at times as the ladies went crazy over a pair of
Swedish wooden clogs and an adorable brass tea kettle. Happily women gave up their bucks for bath products, a large
stainless steel frying pan, ceramic planters, and surprise
packages.

I'll have to admit there were a few peculiar pieces that
had many of us wondering what people might do with them
if purchased. One was a sleek, black, high-heeled shoe tele-
phone. It was something special, for sure. At first glance, I
knew my pre-teen daughter would absolutely love it. As
auctioneer I tried to finagle things my way, but this prize
went to Deb, who was going to present it to her radio-per-
sonality husband on his fiftieth birthday. Perfect.

"Interesting" is the way I'd describe a hunk of marble-
type stuff with a metal, leafy tree sticking out of it. Why
would Marilyn want something like this? Is she off her
rocker? No, she was planning to buy a boy and girl figurine
to place on the metal bench under the metal tree. It would
be a gift for her daughter and son-in-law, whose first kiss
took place on a bench under a tree. The personal touch.

A pair of mannequin legs dressed in shorts had us in
stitches. Half of a body. Yes, this was strange. We all chuckled at the concept of someone actually having these sitting
around the house. We joked about the legs—how they'd
make a good dancing partner, how everybody needs an extra set of legs now and then. On and on we went. Little did
we know that Chris had a plan for this piece of useless
junk. To her it was a treasure she hadn't expected to find.
Her husband collects old uniforms, and guess how they
display them? Incredible! I never would have thunk a person could use mannequin legs!

My pride-and-joy purchase was a battery-operated pepper grinder that shines as it grinds. The potential uses for

this are endless. In the event of a power outage, our newfound pepper grinder could light the way through the veggies and roast beef. Maybe even serve as a reading light—that is, if you don't mind flavorful words. I was so inspired with it, I wrote a little song: "This little pepper grinder of mine—I'm gonna let it shine. This little pepper grinder of mine—I'm gonna let it shine, let it shine, let it shine, let it shine." Anyhow, Steve was thrilled with it, as I knew he would be. When we have dinner guests, the crazy-lady pepper grinder is the highlight of our meal. (Such an exciting life we lead!) Like I said before, one person's trash is another person's treasure.

I've been wondering—what gives an object its value? People frantically collect figurines and Beanie Babies. Others go bonkers over things like Tickle Me Elmo toys, Cabbage Patch dolls, or baseball cards. To some, these items are a prized and cherished treasure. To others, they are a glob of plaster, plastic, mushy material, or cardboard—of no value whatsoever. Why does one flip out over mannequin legs while others would rather have a handy dandy light-your-way pepper grinder? Again I ask—what gives it the value?

This is a deep question, one I'm tossing around in my mind, hoping it will land on an answer that makes sense. The first thing that popped up is that beauty or value is in the eye of the beholder. Another thought is that marketing gives perceived value. Breaking the mold gives value. Being of some use to a person gives value. Then I think of all the great works of art that are extremely valuable, because they are original—the only one of their kind made by the artist. They are priceless and can't be replaced. However, when all is said and done, it's all just stuff—of no eternal value.

Speaking of eternal value, the subject now turns to people. What gives us value? There have been many times in the past when I've felt worthless. A comment or two might have been taken the wrong way, planting the thought within me that I'm no good. I would compare myself to someone who can play the piano like Dino, sing like Sandy Patti, keep house like Martha Stewart, write like Chuck Swindoll, and answer questions like James Dobson. Of course, this person makes their own clothes, has a flawless figure, always wears an engaging smile, has a hilarious sense of humor, a charming personality, and obviously has no problems in life at all. Why do we allow ourselves to wallow like this? Naturally, I was setting myself up for an "I'm no good, I'm worthless, I'm useless, what's the use of even trying to do anything" attitude. My thoughts devalued me. I felt like I wanted to crawl into a garbage can. The only saving factor for me when viewing the "perfect person" was to think that she probably wakes up each morning with a horrendous case of bad breath. After all, almost everybody does.

Something I've learned and am still learning is that I should not do that to myself. It's not wise, it's not healthy, and I'm messing with some pretty serious, stinking thinking. Besides, God doesn't like it. He created me in His image, for a purpose, and He doesn't make any junk.

Each of us was carefully fashioned by the God of the universe. By the One who made the dazzling stars, the majestic mountains, and the plush meadows. We are the handiwork of the Master Artist. A limited edition. An original. The only one of our kind. We have tremendous value and can never be replaced. We are priceless. We come in all shapes and sizes, all colors. Some have freckles; some are missing a few teeth. We have different talents, different ideas, and different directions in life. But we have one thing in common—we are unique.

In John 17 Jesus refers to us as a gift God has given Him. Imagine that! Jesus considers us a cherished gift. If

Jesus thinks that, even has it written in His Word, how can we question it? It is a fact. Jesus values us so much that He prayed for us years before we were born. We are His prized possession. He loves us like no other—even laying down His life on our behalf.

I find that the more I know who I am in Christ—the way He values me and my worth to Him—the less I care about what others think of me, the more I care what He thinks of me, and I change the way I think of myself. I am not worthless. I am not a dud. I can even kick the can! The more I know Him and trust His love, the more I see what a special and unique creature I am. It doesn't matter what people think. It doesn't matter what I think. It matters what Jesus thinks. I am a treasure and so are you.

I praise You because I am fearfully and wonderfully made; Your works are wonderful, I know that full well. (Ps. 129:14)

Potato Words

Fleas. Are you itching yet? I am. The mere mention of them sets a body on fire. Crazy, isn't it? But if you're like me, you're probably scratching your head, your legs, your feet, or all your extremities right now. According to Webster, fleas are small, wingless, bloodsucking insects that feed on warm-blooded animals. Argggghhhhh!

Our kitty, Oreo, "the elephant cat," was acting strangely. Abnormally abnormal. She kept chewing and biting herself. Huge hunks of her hair were falling out. Open sores covered her bald spots. She was clearly uncomfortable. We wondered if she was sick or maybe having mental problems. We were confused, not knowing what to do. Finally, someone suggested that she might have fleas. The thought had never occurred to us. Denial set in. "Certainly not. Impossible. She's an indoor cat."

After hearing the idea, I was hesitant. Did I really want to know the truth? Apprehensively I gazed upon her, looking for clues, inspecting her with Sherlock Holmes intensity. Carefully I made my way through her forest of fur, and instantly I found evidence of insect infestation. Oh, yuck! Let me tell you right now, I was totally grossed out! Oreo's body was riddled with those disgusting bloodsuckers, and I'm not joking. Poor kitty. And to think we accused her of being wacko!

Naturally, this unwelcome discovery came in the evening, right before we climbed into bed. My imagination ran wild, feeding me with farfetched ideas. *Fleas are using my bed as their trampoline, doing back flips, whirly twirls, and forward rolls. Then they're gonna jump from my pillow to my head and use my hair as their restroom facilities. They're swimming in the carpet, ready to dive on unsuspecting ankles and legs. They've buried themselves in the couch cushions, chomping at the bit to chomp mine. They're playing patty-cake with Jesse's stuffed animals. They're hopping from room to room in hopes of hijacking a box elder bug to get to higher territory. In fact, I'm sure I saw one piggybacking a ride up the curtain. Every nook and cranny of the house is infested. They're probably in my toothbrush, for crying out loud! I just know they want to suck every last bit of blood and guts from my body!*

I had a full-blown case of the heebie jeebies, not wanting to touch or look at anything too closely. My, how the mind doth create!

After a very restless and itchy night, I awoke with renewed determination to tackle the problem. Maybe I could find a secret button to push and make these pesky varmints disappear. Unfortunately, it would be a bit more involved than that. Steve took a trip to the nearby vet's office, returning with ointments for Oreo and sprays and foggers for the house. We were faced with a lot of work and an outlay of money. Oreo needed to be treated. The house needed to be bombed. Then everything would need to be washed, scrubbed, sprayed, and disinfected. After all that, we'd still question whether we got them all. How can a little bitty thing like that cause such great problems?

I thought of something else that is small, wingless, and bloodsucking that feeds on warm-blooded animals. Our tongue. It can cause destruction, be full of deadly poison, and, in a way, bite like a flea. One definition of fleabite is— "a trifling pain or annoyance." Tongues and fleabites can be similar indeed.

The words we say can hurt or heal. They can cause great pain or give needed encouragement. They can tear someone down or build someone up. At times, the words we use remind me of how we verbally abuse the potato. Consider its plight. The potato is covered in dirt from day one. When it finally emerges to see the light of day, we poke or gouge out its eyes. We peel it, cut it up, boil it, whip it, mash it, or smash it. Other times we fry it, bake it, or twice bake it to double the torture. We drown it in butter, sour cream, or gravy. The poor potato doesn't stand a chance! Our words can do to people what we do to potatoes. "You're no good. Why can't you ever get it right? You'll never amount to anything. There's no way you can do that. Why don't you just give up? You're fat! You're hopeless. Forget even trying." Fleabite, fleabite, fleabite. "Potato words" and fleabites result in a need for damage control. Once words are out of our mouths, they are gone for good. There's no taking them back. "Potato words" plant themselves deep within the recipient's soul and produce a crop of negative feelings and emotional scars.

But then, look at honey. It is soothing, calms the soul, and is used for medicinal purposes. Honey's sweet flavor brings delight to the lips. Honey drips. It lingers. It's like candy—nice and smooth. In fact, honey is used as an endearing term. Have you ever heard anyone called "potato?" Stud, yes. Spud, no. "Honey words" go down much easier and are more palatable than "potato words." "I know you can do it. Hang in there. How can I help you? You are a beautiful woman of God. God really blessed me when He put you in my life. I'm praying for you. I love you." Which would you rather hear?

I recently read a little ditty that told of a group of frogs traveling through the woods. Two of them fell into a deep pit and all the other frogs gathered around. When they saw how deep the pit was, they told the two frogs that they were as good as dead. The two frogs ignored the comments and tried with all of their might to jump out of the pit. The other frogs kept telling them to stop, that they didn't have a chance, that they were as good as dead. Finally, one of the frogs took heed of what the other frogs were saying and gave up. He fell down and died. The other frog continued to jump as hard as he could. Once again, the crowd of frogs yelled at him to stop the pain and just die. He jumped even harder and finally made it out. When he got out, the other frogs said, "Didn't you hear us?" The frog explained to them that he was deaf. He thought they were encouraging him the entire time.

From this we learn that there is the power of life and death in the tongue. A "honey word" to someone who is down can lift them up and help them make it through the day. A "potato word" to someone who is down can put them over the edge and destroy them. Be careful with your words. Next time you're itching to say something, think.

Reckless words pierce like a sword, but the tongue of the wise brings healing. (Prov. 12:18)

Toenail Love

You want me to do what? Cut your toenails! Are you nuts?"

Feet smell, and after you touch them so does your hand. The typical progression goes like this: The foot is handled, transferring the odor to your fingertips. Your nose starts to itch (of course), so it must be scratched. Okay, you can guess what's next. The aroma of this lower extremity is now implanted at the tip of your nostrils to breathe in and out all day long. It's bad enough when the scent belongs to you, but when it's someone else's? I really don't care to be associated with this scenario.

I have to admit that I've been faced with this unpleasantry on more occasions than I'd like. Because of my husband's frequent bouts with back pain, there were many times when he was physically unable to carry out the important task of toenail trimming, leaving me as the prime candidate to perform this procedure. (I'd like to interject here that his toenails are not a pretty sight, and I've never had the desire to embrace them!)

Examining Proverbs 31 left me clueless as to whether or not the Virtuous Woman pruned the nails on her husband's little piggies, but while researching this matter thoroughly I stumbled across a few verses from the "Pedicure Paraphrase" that gave me the sought-after answers:

Verse 11: . . . her husband has full confidence in her *clipping ability.*

Verse 12: . . . she brings him good, not bad *shaped toenails*, all the days of her life.

Verse 23: Her husband is respected at the city gate *because of his well-groomed feet.*

Verse 29: Many women do noble things, *but you cut your husband's toenails!*

Actually, I'm storytelling here. (Was it obvious?) These new and revised verses aren't what the original author had in mind. However, if he had penned Proverbs 31 when his back was hurting and his toenails were overgrown, he might have worded it accordingly.

Anyhow, my husband, amazed that I would stoop so low, proudly proclaimed my efforts. (Wow! It's like the Virtuous Woman after all! In verse twenty-eight, her husband praises her.) Steve announced to anyone who would listen, "It's a true sign of love when your wife cuts your toenails for you." Isn't that charming? Personally, I'd prefer not to include love and toenails in the same breath!

I wonder—could there be a lesson in this for me? I remember when Jesus stooped lower than a Jewish servant to wash His disciples' dirty, rotten, stinking feet. Seems He was trying to teach them something about humility and love. In fact, I can almost hear Him saying, "Guys, watch

Me here. Try to get this through your heads. True greatness means being a servant to others."

Okay, Lord, I get the point.

I have set you an example that you should do as I have done for you. (John 13:15)

Born to Sell

I was born to sell. Yes, you read it right: sell, not shop. Hand me any item and, if I believe in it, I can sell it. I simply let the product sell itself by showcasing its fine features.

Selling is in my blood, ingrained since birth. As a baby, I sold kisses for a smile, instantly fulfilling all sales quotas. My dad was a salesman extraordinaire. Growing up I automatically developed his style, his lingo, his charisma, and his panache. Throughout my childhood, marketing became as natural and pleasurable to me as watching cartoons.

Each year my mom planted a huge garden and each year it yielded a bountiful crop. Succulent, sun-kissed tomatoes. Tender green beans picked in their prime. Golden ears of corn—Iowa's best—every kernel bursting with sweet, creamy flavor. Rhubarb. Zucchini. Green peppers. You name it. The surplus, after canning and freezing, was mine to sell. Door to door I traveled, peddling my wares. I was a walking farmer's market. After every trip I returned with empty arms and pockets overflowing with profits.

Other times I created a makeshift vegetable stand on the sidewalk with a folding chair and card table. The leaves of the towering oak tree shaded me from the intensity of the summer sun. A baby scale to weigh the produce, bags to hold my customers' purchases, and an old cigar box for a cash register were stationed on the table. The tantalizing food and my eye-catching signs lured people in passing vehicles. I offered service with a smile, the best product in town, and deals that couldn't be beat. My grade school charm was irresistible.

On various occasions I walked from block to block taking orders for Girl Scout cookies or candy or fruit for the band. My sales volume always exceeded that of my peers. I was motivated, because I was born to sell.

Believe it or not, there was actually a time I tried to sell rocks to my neighbors. These weren't your ordinary rocks; they were specially hand-painted by me, then age six or seven. Innocently, I expected everyone to buy my creations because they were so fascinating. (This was before the "pet rock" craze.) I believed in the unique qualities of my products and was determined to sell them. Certain neighbors saw the great potential of these colorful stones, too, and made a purchase; others just paid me to keep the rock. Either way, I was successful. (Today I wonder whether my parents even knew I did this.)

One day I advanced to the realm of porch sales, holding them on a regular basis. As a salesman for a superior line of stainless steel cookware, my dad occasionally took lesser grade pots and pans as trade-ins toward the purchase of a set of his merchandise. This gave me an ongoing supply of odds and ends for my little "shop." Customers aware of the procedure knew that if they checked back periodically they would find a different variety of goods on display. I had well-seasoned cast iron skillets and Dutch ovens, aluminum pots and pans, copper-bottomed stainless steel pieces, non-stick products, electric frying pans, coffee pots, and even some complete sets of high-priced, quality cookware. The selection was always changing and always exciting— meeting the needs of campers, newlyweds, and the general public. As a kid who knew my product well, I thoroughly enjoyed sending away satisfied customers.

From my porch sales revenues, baby-sitting, and taking orders for furry little creatures I made ("its" and "things"), I saved enough money in three months to accompany my parents on a Scandinavian trip. My dad had won the trip through a sales contest, and naturally I asked if I could go along. At first, he said, "No," but I persisted as any twelve-year-old would. Finally, he relented, but insisted I pay my own way. My youthful determination paid off, and I joined Mom and Dad after working hard to earn the hundreds of dollars.

Years later, my husband and I opened a Christian bookstore. I loved selling products that were designed to bring people closer to God. I delighted in presenting the wonderful features of the various Bibles available. I enthusiastically sold books that had the ability to change lives. With excitement, I explained which music or rental videos would best meet our customers' needs. What joy it brought me knowing that our products helped hurting hearts, reached lost souls, and built up and supported the Christian community. The merchandise we represented made a tremendous impact for the kingdom of God.

We don't have our store any longer, but I still represent Someone very important. He is Someone I really believe in. Everyday I want to showcase His fine features. Hopefully people around me can see His characteristics shining through my life and realize they can't live without Him.

We are, in a sense, marketing agents for Jesus Christ. The way we represent Him can either turn people toward Him or away from Him. I'm trying to keep my marketing skills polished and am determined to be successful. Are you?

Let your light shine before men, that they may see your good deeds and praise your Father in heaven. (Matt. 5:16)

A New Wardrobe

Clothing styles are something else these days, aren't they? I get my jollies watching the never-ending parade of the uniquely clad public. It makes for an entertaining way to wait for traffic lights to change or to amuse myself while shopping. At my kids' school events I get an eyeful. It seems today's fashions cover a broad spectrum of shapes, sizes, materials, and ugliness. Almost anything goes. Some people use their garb to make a statement. Many want to make an exclamation point. Others just leave a question mark in the viewer's mind, like "What was she thinking when she put that on?" One thing's for sure, though. We all need clothes, and it's our choice what kind we're gonna wear.

Have you ever noticed that people carry themselves and act according to the way they're dressed? Some people present themselves in an extravagant fashion—exquisitely tailored. Their mere presence and actions exude confidence and high self-esteem. Those in "slob-o-la" threads—pants that are three sizes too big, six inches too long, and frayed and worn through in places—are naturally going to slouch

168 GOTTA GET 'EM FIXED!

along. Then you might have a woman dressed in biblical clothing—lo(w) and behold—with the almost-had-a-dress-on look. Of course, the woman has to take itty bitty steps, because if she over extends her stride by one iota with that figure-enhancing, stretchy, spandex fabric, something might let loose and she'll go flying across the room like a rubber band stretched over a finger. But, you know what? Her goal of attracting attention will definitely be accomplished.

Losing some weight left me in a dilemma, forcing me to update my wardrobe after years of wearing the same old stuff. I was at the point where I felt frumpy—all my clothes were several sizes too big. I wanted to be pretty, to let the world experience me in a new way. It was time for a different look. But, with garment styles running the gamut, I was confused and wondered what I should do. Where would I begin? What style would suit me best? Even the tiniest dressing decision overwhelmed me.

Grabbing a catalog, I figured the easiest and most informative process would be to have everything laid out in pictures before me. That way I could choose my new look from a wide range of styles and colors and even have an idea how it would appear. The descriptives with the pictures excited me. Who wouldn't want something that claimed to drape attractively, to be sheer elegance, flattering, or striking? Or maybe I should go the versatile, great for play, easy to wear, comfortable, breathable, stain-release route. Actually, I didn't have much of a choice; I needed it all. So I plodded through the pages of the catalog, pondering the problem at hand.

Ads for tummy control, hip slimmer, thigh trimmer, and inches off piqued my interest. Then questions flooded my mind. What would happen if I wore all these features at one time? Where would all the extra me go? When something is squeezed in one spot, it's gonna sneak out elsewhere. It would be like trying to pour a twelve-ounce Coke into a ten-ounce glass. The extra two ounces have to go somewhere, so they spill out all over the place. I pictured this happening to me. I would either have a large inner-tube-type roll around my midsection, protruding beyond my chest and wobbling ostentatiously, or my eyes would bulge out. Neither one is a pretty sight. Besides, it's not me. If I'm going to show off my curves, I'd rather they be my normal lumps than to have people think I forgot to take off my swim toy before getting dressed.

When I flipped to the undergarment section of the catalog, bewilderment set in. I have a hard enough time trying to make ordinary, everyday decisions, but when seeing I had to choose between a white bra and a cappuccino bra I didn't know if I could handle the pressure. I just knew that if I chose the cappuccino bra I'd be asked if I wanted French vanilla, hazelnut cream, or mocha. What are they thinking of when they come up with colors? I scanned the entire catalog and couldn't find another article of clothing listed in cappuccino. Why bras? Then it hit me, and I realized this made perfect sense. You see, bras have cups, and cups hold cappuccino. Simple, isn't it? I'm afraid, though, that now at restaurants I might absentmindedly try ordering a cappuccino in size DD. Or, knowing me, if a waitress asks if I'd like some cappuccino, I might respond with, "No thanks, I already have two cups." For the time being, I think I'll stick with white bras.

That was only the beginning of the clothing color crisis. I came across mocha, celery, butter, plum, cream, olive, lime, sage, strawberry, mango, melon, tangerine, mustard, and grape, among others. Then there were camel and leopard. I decided that by the time I got down the fruit aisle, veggie aisle, condiment aisle, and dairy aisle in the grocery store, and then headed over to the zoo to compare colors before I could order anything, I'd be better off purchasing my clothes in a department store where I could see everything up close and personal. I didn't know what size I wore anyway, so it would be next to impossible to order a new wardrobe sight unseen.

Laying the catalog aside, I courageously hopped in the car and drove to the mall. Once there my confidence dissipated, and I timidly entered a clothing store as a friendly sales associate approached me. She didn't have a clue what she was in for when she asked, "Can I help you?" I immediately dropped to my knees and tightly engulfed her ankles in my arms. "Please, please, please," I begged, "I don't know what to do. I don't know where to begin. I haven't bought clothes for years. I've lost a lot of weight and don't even know what size I wear anymore. I need everything. Please, please help me! Make me beautiful."

I'm sure she was thinking, *hey, lady, we sell clothes; we don't do miracles!* but she spared me her thoughts. She saw my desperation, and the brave soul became my personal attendant for the entire evening.

After making me feel at home in a changing room, my new "best friend" went about the business of recreating me. Back and forth she traipsed, carrying armloads of dresses, pants, skirts, and shirts for me to try. As I primped, twirled, and evaluated myself in front of the mirror, my helper cheered me on. "Rah, rah, siss boom bah! The red looks great, but the gray is blah!" The hours passed and clothes piled up. Practically everything in the store made its way through the doors of my new residence. I tried on, I tried on, and I tried on, even styles I normally wouldn't have given a second glance. Some articles were clearly not for me, but others were a pleasant surprise. By closing time, I had a wonderful new wardrobe. Of course, I was also encouraged to get all the add-ons—matching earrings, a fancy scarf, socks, and pantyhose—the works. I felt great. I could hardly wait to show off the new and improved me.

Next began the process of weeding out the old clothes from my closet. I wouldn't want or need to wear them again. After all, they didn't fit and really weren't my style any longer. I sure didn't need them cluttering up my closet, but I just couldn't bear to get rid of everything. I clung to a few odds and ends like a toddler with his favorite stuffed animal. It's amazing how those old things have a sneaky way of jumping out of the closet and mingling with my new outfits in the name of accessorizing. Even though the shirts are big and bulky, I wear them over my jumpers or with jeans. Some things are hard to give up.

Many years ago I dressed in horrible fashion. My clothing was hideous on me and people seemed to be repelled by it. Then someone introduced me to the Master Tailor. He sized me up, looked me over real good, and said, "You need some work. I'm gonna fix you up right. You see, child, that old garb you're wearing—the anger, bitterness, pride, selfishness, envy, jealousy, strife, hatred, and other things—doesn't fit you well anymore. It's old. It's outdated. It's ugly. Really, it could be considered downright repulsive.

"Now that you've come to Me, you're going to dress like Me. I'll wardrobe you with clothes made from the same pattern as Mine. You'll love the way they never go out of style. In fact, the longer you wear them the better they look. And, best of all, they are fashions that are guaranteed to fit."

The Master Tailor then proceeded to outfit me. He grabbed all the essential pieces in the choicest fabrics and personally attended to my apparel needs. "Look in the mirror, Twila. Doesn't that compassion look great on you? Couple that with some coordinating kindness and humility, and then throw on some gentleness, patience, and forgiveness. Wow! We're getting somewhere here! This is a good look for you. Let's pull the whole ensemble together with a blazer of love and top it off with a hat of gratitude and thankfulness. Twila, you look beautiful! This wardrobe suits you to a T. You are definitely a new creation!

"Now I want the world to experience the new you. Hold your head high, carry yourself confidently with grace, and put a big smile on your face, because you're wearing Designer's clothes. Just make sure you throw away all the old stuff, and don't even think of keeping anything for accessorizing. It will ruin the whole look."

You were taught, with regard to your former way of life, to put off your old self, which is being corrupted by its deceitful desires; to be made new in the attitude of your minds; and to put on the new self, created to be like God in true righteousness and holiness. (Eph. 4:22–24)

No Comprendo

To borrow a line from the author of Proverbs: "There are three things that are too amazing for me, four things that I don't understand."

Why do people ask ridiculous questions? They notice something has changed about you so they say, "You look different. Did you get a haircut?" In actuality, the change they've noticed is weight loss. When asked this, one of my normal responses might be, "No, I've just shaved off my mustache!" Then there are those who are really observant—the ones who ask if we've lost a little weight because our face looks thinner. That's right, folks! We could lose 100 pounds and the only place it shows up is our face. Maybe it's that intense physical training we give it by constantly flapping our jaws.

Another thing I can't figure out is a tag on my blue jeans that states, "Wash and dry separately." How could you wash *and* dry them at the same time?

Or, the message on the back of my lip balm container: "This product has not been tested on animals." I'm sorry,

173

but why would furry little creatures need to wear lip balm? To make them more appealing to their mates? Since reading this, every time I use the product I get depressed thinking about the poor critters that will never experience the joy of soft, supple lips.

Last on my list for now is the label on the Robitussin bottle. This medication claims it will help you have a "productive" cough. Do I really want to know what a productive cough is? What kinds of things will it produce? Phlegm? Fur balls? Fruit?

Speaking of producing fruit, I'm reminded that Jesus wants our lives to do just that. (Wasn't that smooth how I tied Robitussin and fruit together?) However, there is no magical syrup to swallow that enables us to "cough it up." I've found that the more I focus on Christ, and the more time I spend in God's Word and in prayer, the more I naturally produce godly fruit. With Jesus providing the light, the Scriptures fertilizing, and prayer watering, my life has the essentials for being productive.

While I was recovering from a motor vehicle accident a few years ago, I received a package in the mail from my sister-in-law's niece, Rachel. Included with a get-well card were some coloring books and a box of crayons. A note read,

> Dear Twila,
> Remember me? Barely I'm sure, but I sure do remember you showing me the fine art of coloring and telling me it was OK for grown ups, too. I still do color for relaxation on busy days, and I'll be 23 soon. . . .

Wow! This "teaching moment" happened many years ago, but it evidently made a lasting impression on Rachel. Something very unimportant that I had done (and not even remembered) influenced her life. I began to wonder—what things of significance am I leaving behind that people will remember years from now? What kind of fruit am I bearing? Is it fruit that will last?

A twenty-three-year-old woman remembers that I taught her to color as a child, but does she remember any lessons I left behind for her about the Lord? Did I leave any? What kind of impact am I having now on people's lives? Am I making the most of every opportunity God gives me?

The box of crayons and coloring books were an eye opener for me. When I am gone from this earth, I hope others will have lasting memories of what I produced— God's fruit.

I chose you and appointed you to go and bear fruit— fruit that will last. (John 15:16)

It Shows

My former pastor laughed as he remembered an incident at one of his previous churches. He shared how the lively choir director enthusiastically led her group of singers in joyful song. As she raised her arms, her half-slip inched its way down, down, down. (Now we know why it's called a slip!) Some in this situation would act embarrassed or as if in a fix, but not this fearless female. The slip, now puddled around her pumps, was flicked off her feet with flare as a stunned pastor stared in disbelief. Amazingly, she didn't miss a beat, and the song was finished with gusto. Because the choir loft was partitioned off, this potential cause for an epidemic of giggles and guffaws was not apparent to worshipers. Pastor, however, fought to maintain his composure in front of the clueless congregation, especially after the choir director nonchalantly picked up the discarded undergarment and marched off with it tucked under her arm, almost as if it were an everyday occurrence. This was definitely a case of "Excuse me, miss, but your slip is showing."

I heard a story about two nuns taking a Sunday afternoon drive down a winding country road. Farmhouses dotted the flowing fields. Corn tassels glistened in the sun's mid-day glow. Amber waves of grain danced across the fruited plains. (After all, this is America!) It was a perfect day for a ride—that is until their car ran out of fuel. Being in the country caused a crisis. There were no filling stations nearby, so the nuns set out to find the closest homestead. After a small jaunt, the sisters happened upon a place. A few taps on the door brought a kindly farmer in response.

"Sir, we just ran out of gas and wondered if you might be able to help us."

"It would be my pleasure, ladies. There's only one problem. I have gas to give you but nothing to carry it in except a bed pan."

The sisters assured the good man that they were perfectly okay with this plan. They were just thrilled to find gas in the middle of nowhere. The nuns walked back to their car and began filling the gas tank when a gentleman drove beside and stopped. "Ladies," he said, "I'm not of your denomination, but I sure do admire your faith."

This very-possibly-true-but-maybe-not example of "don't look now, but your faith is showing" made me think about how we are constantly being watched. People notice what we do and how we react in different situations, even when we are unaware. I have experienced many circumstances in which people were blown away by my faith. They didn't know how I could go through certain traumatic times and seem not to be affected by them. They admired the overwhelming peace and joy I had. What they saw was God's grace in action as a result of my faith. He gets all the glory.

I'll have to admit, though, there are times when I have a really hard time keeping myself in check. My old nature cries from my core, "Let me out or I'll explode!" These are the times I struggle with how my testimony appears to others. I can handle crisis situations pretty well: give me a son with a ruptured appendix, a car accident, a death, any of the tough stuff, and—with God's help and a truckload of grace—people see a solid faith. But give me a trashed out house full of half-finished chores, three children whining at the same time, or a baseball game (yes, a baseball game), and I want to go ballistic. These are the times that try a mom's soul.

One particular game comes to mind that was a true test of my Christianity. It was the night my son's team played the Big Dogs. The Big Dog name served them well, because they thought they were. After each strike he pitched, the Dog on the mound strutted through the infield like a rooster. His coach and teammates egged him on. It was quite the show. Then things quickly deteriorated from there. They began mocking, provoking, and poking fun at the boys on our team. A group of teens in the stands near me began cheering the pitcher, encouraging him to hit the batter with his pitches. In my concerned motherly way (after I couldn't take any more of it), I said, "Guys, don't tell the pitcher to hit the batter. How would you like it if you were batting and someone told the pitcher to hit you?" I was proud of myself, thinking I handled the twerps quite well, in spite of what I really wanted to say. But then another mom yelled, "Yeah, that's my son batting! How would you like it if I called your pitcher a beached whale? Well, he is!" Oh, oh! Things were eroding fast. It was apparent that our fans were becoming infuriated. Before I knew it, the Big Dog attitude was spreading like an elephant's diarrhea—it was all over the park! An ugly sight, and it stunk, too.

The small simmer in me was swiftly changing to a full, raging boil. My blood pressure elevated to stroke level. I was doing everything within my power to keep my mouth shut, but the steam started to escape through my ears. I was clearly agitated—on the edge of explosion. Rapidly I paced the grounds, trying to release some tension so that I could remain Christ-like. At that point, my thoughts turned to the Scriptures. *Pride comes before a fall.* I pled with the Lord to make that come true, and soon! I found myself praying a paraphrase of Psalm 3:7: *Arise, O Lord! Deliver my son's team, O my God! Strike all the Big Dogs on the jaw; break the teeth of those who are wicked.* The temptation to traipse into the Big Dog dugout to turn them all into toy poodles flickered in my mind. I could have gotten into real trouble if I had unleashed my caged emotions, but watching others who caved to human nature made me thankful that God had been recreating me over the years.

I learned several things that day. First, and foremost, I can't stand cocky twits! Second, I should memorize more imprecatory Psalms. And third, I need to always have an attitude that shows my faith in Christ. I came close to giving a negative testimony that day. When I think about how capable I was of stoning the other team, I scare myself. People aren't drawn into God's family that way. Christ is in me, even at baseball games, and others should see Him in me, regardless of the circumstances. That was a little too close for comfort.

Now my thoughts go to the book of Acts, where a real stoning took place. Saul, serving as a coat rack, stood by as Stephen was stoned to death. Stephen's Spirit-controlled response to his torturers and the way he handled his pain and pressure were well observed by Saul. Saul, who later became Paul, never forgot it. Eventually Saul/Paul saw the light and became a follower of Jesus Christ.

Later, Paul and his buddy, Silas, caused an uproar in Philippi. They were dragged before the magistrates and then stripped, severely beaten, and thrown into prison (a regular occurrence for Paul). Guards carefully watched Paul and Silas, whose feet were fastened in stocks. At midnight, these two crazy Christians carried on by praying and singing hymns to God. All the other prisoners listened to them. It was the ultimate concert. In fact, as they were singing, the earth began to shake, rattle, and roll. (And Elvis wasn't even there!) The prison doors flew open, and everybody's chains came loose.

The jailer was terrified and prepared to kill himself rather than face the shame of having prisoners escape. Just then Paul called out, "Whoa, boy! Don't hurt yourself. We're all still here." I'm sure the jailer was shocked. Paul and Silas could have fled to freedom, but instead remained where they were. What a testimony! The jailer approached them and said, "Excuse me, sirs, but your faith is showing. What must I do to be saved?" Not only did the prison doors open wide, but also spiritual doors opened wide to share the Gospel with the jailer, his whole household, and a lot of prisoners.

By showing faith in trying circumstances we are being used as vessels that can bring others closer to God. Maybe instead of praying for fewer trials so that we might witness better, we should pray that we might witness better through our trials. When was the last time someone said to you, "Excuse me, miss, but your faith is showing"?

Whatever happens, conduct yourselves in a manner worthy of the gospel of Christ. (Phil. 2:27a)

The Fishin' Foot

These feet were made for fishin'. No, I'm not writing a new country and western song. I've just come to the realization that I have dual-purpose feet.

A while back I had a cyst removed from my foot and a bunionectomy performed. This is a surgical procedure that involves opening up your foot, cutting away part of the bone, and placing a temporary steel pin inside to hold things together correctly. Unfortunately, this left me confined to my recliner unable to do housework (too bad) and required others to wait on me hand and foot (pun intended). Also, my husband and friends had to care for our then twelve-month-old "little man," who left a whirlwind of destruction wherever he went.

Day in and day out I reclined in my favorite living room chair, propping my foot on a pile of pillows. My foot smiled back at me, swaddled in neon pink coverings, and gave me fuel for my creative thought process. It's a rough life, but how do you think I was able to start writing this book?

After four days, I returned to the doctor to get my foot rewrapped with fresh dressing. I was excited! I had noticed a rainbow of purple, blue, green, and yellow colors peeking out from under my bandage, but now I'd be able to experience first hand the blood, the guts, and the gore lurking beneath.

As the doctor carefully and gently removed the blood-stained gauze, my foot was exposed. On the left side of my foot, protruding through some stitches, was the steel pin, bent and shaped to resemble a hook. Two rows of stitches, meticulously criss-crossed and knotted with a special thread or line, swam in a sea of bruises. Instantly, my overly imaginative brain engaged. When I remembered that my foot hadn't been washed for several days, I envisioned it as a hook, line, and stinker. (Sorry, I couldn't resist!) I was suddenly aware that I had a dual-purpose foot. I now had a fishin' foot!

Enter my little world of make believe with me and observe as a delightful fish story unfolds:

What a glorious day! The sun burst its brilliance through the fluffy, cotton-candy clouds dotting the soft blue sky. Songbirds chirped their joyful melodies in harmony with the rustling leaves of nearby trees. The water, glistening, mirrored the beauty of the heavens. My golden tresses and white seersucker dress gently blew in the light breeze. I sat on the weather-worn dock, sipping iced tea from its sweating glass, as my bare feet dangled over the edge, swaying back and forth in the refreshingly cool water. There I waited, anticipating my great catch. I knew the blue gill and sunfish would soon be kissing my foot, nibbling away at the juicy worm woven onto its hook. How could the little creatures resist my new and improved fishin' foot?

As you can see, my thoughts have a tendency to wander. Anyhow, this far-out fantasy brought to mind the day Jesus watched Simon and Andrew casting their nets into the lake. He said to the brothers, "I want you to follow Me and start fishin' for men." In other words, "You've got dual-purpose feet. Get your fishin' feet ready; you have a lot of ground to cover. Bait your hooks with the Good News and let men, women, and children start chewing on it. Be ready to give them a full course dinner. Hopefully, when you get to heaven, you'll have some great fish stories to tell."

Jesus, in giving the Great Commission, had this same desire for us. I don't know about you, but I'd better bait my hook. I've got some fishin' to do.

How beautiful are the feet of those who bring good news! (Rom. 10:15b)

Garbage Can Freedom

There is great freedom in owning a garbage can. Before you think I've trashed my brains, let me offer an explanation.

Several years ago our city administrators were in a tizzy because they hadn't written their annual quota of new laws. They brainstormed and created a regulation requiring the townsfolk to cough up more of their hard-earned money, but in a very inconvenient way. The light bulbs went on in their noggins and visions of garbage stickers danced in their heads. Yes, garbage stickers. We would now be expected to purchase little orange stickers and attach them to each bag of garbage we set out on trash pick-up day. Another option was to purchase a larger, red, one-year sticker to fasten to our garbage can. Without the special adhesives we would no longer receive rubbish removal benefits. Keep in mind that this service was previously covered by our property taxes.

Call him stubborn or rebellious, but my husband absolutely refused to comply with the hassle and extra expense of this new ruling. In other words, we would find a new way to rid ourselves of the refuse.

At first we had a dumpster available to us at the site of our Christian bookstore in a nearby town. This worked fairly well, but it involved loading up and transporting our trash to another location. No problem. At least we weren't forced to do something against our will.

When we closed our store we no longer had the convenience of the dumpster. Ah, but we had a contingency plan. We would burn. A backyard blaze would add excitement to an otherwise humdrum life. Now we could experience the warm feelings associated with cozy fires on a regular basis. Who knows? Maybe we could even sing, "It only takes a spark to get a fire going" as we fueled the flames. And, there's nothing quite like an ooey-gooey marshmallow perfectly toasted over a trash heap!

But before long we had a dilemma. Sometimes it rained. Sometimes there were blustery winds. Sometimes it snowed. Sometimes somebody just didn't feel up to burning. That was okay, though. We have a big garage.

Let me try to give you an appreciation for what some wives deal with. Are you ready for this?

We have dirty diapers accumulating in a Diaper Genie. Have you ever seen one of those? You put a poopy Pampers in the canister, give the lid a twist or two, and the Genie miraculously seals it in plastic. Repeat the process over and over and you have a whole string of diapers individually encased, appearing amazingly similar to overgrown frankfurters. I call them my Diaper Genie wienies. Diaper Genies are great for normal purposes, but I don't think the diaper wienies were meant to decay for five months before being discarded. We have diaper wienies.

Next, we have a trash compactor. My husband, magical man that he is, can get about two months of waste products crushed down to the consistency of a cement block. We try to use the compactor for non-food items, but every once in a while an unknowing guest will slip in some savory scraps. Yes, they begin to stink! Now we have diaper wienies *and* trash compactor bags.

Well, there are some things you just don't put into trash compactors or into the recycle bin, so they must go into the receptacle located in the pantry. A sample of those items would be paper plates dripping with excess edibles, wet diapers, onion tops, egg shells, coffee grounds, light bulbs, aerosol cans, or anything else like that. Since the garbage bags used in this container are "kitchen size," they reach capacity rapidly. More bags to take outside. Meanwhile, diaper wienies, trash compactor bags, *and* pantry rubbish collect. But remember, we have a big garage!

Oh, I forgot to point out the three bathrooms, four bedrooms, office, rec room, family room, and other locations amassing the discarded debris—including used kitty litter! Either the garage was getting smaller or the towering trash was taking over. We had it all—pungent piles, malodorous mounds, stenchy stacks, reeking rubbish, decomposed dodo, rotting refuse. Are you starting to get the drift? (P.U.— it's pretty bad!)

Finally, a day comes along with no wind, rain, or snow. Motivation sets in. Hallelujah! One load at a time, heaped high on the dolly, makes its way to the burn pile. Okay, let's throw it all in the fire! Not so easy. We must not forget that some things cannot be incinerated or are too compacted to burn properly. Therefore the bags are rooted through individually and stuff is sorted as the inferno rages. Plastic? Rubber? Metal? It'll melt or burn—eventually. So will diaper wienies, after three or four days. Better watch out for the aerosol cans and light bulbs, though!

Another problem arises. Max, the wonder dog, decides our neighbors should participate in the celebration with us. He then devises a plan to distribute the charred debris throughout the neighborhood. After all, God says share.

Pardon me for asking this, but wouldn't it have been a whole lot easier to buy those stupid stickers in the first place? I'm sorry, but after months and months of this routine, I had to break free from the bondage. I told my husband that we *would* have a garbage can, and it *would* have a sticker on it. Some things just aren't worth the fight.

Garbage cans are blessings, and there is great freedom in owning one. These days whenever we take out a bag of garbage we both do a little deliverance dance. So does our garage.

One thing I've noticed since obtaining a garbage can—it doesn't do us any good if it's not deposited at the end of our driveway on Thursday mornings. Forgetting this one simple step causes the "pile syndrome" again. Our garbage must be disposed of and removed on a regular basis.

It's kind of like the garbage we pile up in our lives—the pungent pride, stinking stubbornness, trashy talk, or other smelly stuff. If our personal piles aren't dealt with and disposed of as we become aware of them, they tend to fester and grow. The more they grow, the more out of control and unbearable they become. Our garbage starts affecting us and the people around us negatively.

The good news is God has made a way to rid us of our rubbish. We just need to willingly take our trash to Jesus, dump it at His feet, and He will dispose of it for us. He will remove it as far as the east is from the west, never to be seen again. He will replace the stench with a pleasing aroma that only Christ can give. Such joy! Such relief! And, do you know what the best part of doing this is? There are no little stickers involved. God's garbage removal service is absolutely free!

As far as the east is from the west, so far has He removed our transgressions from us. (Ps. 103:12)

Choices

To be or not to be? Coffee, tea, or milk? Dine in or take out? French fries or baked potato? To supersize or not to supersize? Perennials or annuals? Chicago Cubs or St. Louis Cardinals? News on channel six or news on channel eight? The pink dress or the red dress? Choices. Our lives are bombarded with them.

Remember that crazy, old TV show "Let's Make a Deal"? Monty Hall, the host, scanned the audience of hyper, outrageously dressed guests and selected enthusiastic folks to wheel and deal with him. Monty always presented these guests with a barrage of choices. Often, he would pull out a wad of $100 bills and say, "You can take $1,000, or you can trade it for this, that, or the other thing." Later in the show he might offer a trade for what was behind door #1, door #2, or door #3, maybe even giving them a peek to whet their appetite. Of course, the doors looked equally appealing and enticing. Many times the ecstatic guest became the proud owner of a sparkling washer and dryer or a beautiful luxury vehicle. Other times the choice gained a billy goat or a broken down jalopy.

I could never understand why I despised grocery shopping, until one day the cause of stress hit me – too many choices! Each of my grocery excursions normally lasted a couple of hours and in the past seemed to always bring on a good case of stomach duress. That's why I try to keep my trips down to once a month or less. Think about it. There are probably twenty or thirty decisions to make on each item you buy. Large, medium, small, or teeny tiny. Expensive, a little more expensive, or really expensive. Cans, plastic, or glass. Chopped, minced, mashed, refried, stewed, or pureed. With sugar, no sugar added, or tasteless. Red, green, or black. Fat free, light, one third less fat, or the good stuff. And, if you add in the countless brands you have to muddle through, you've got some heavy-duty thinking to do. Then there's the fear that the world might come to an end if I purchase the wrong bottle of pancake syrup!

I admit that the choices I make at the grocery store aren't going to change the course of history. Unless, of course, I buy chunky peanut butter to spread on the celery sticks I'm serving the president, and when biting into one he breaks his tooth because the shell wasn't properly removed from the peanut, which creates the need for him to have emergency dental work, causing him to miss his very important fundraising campaign meeting that will determine whether or not he wins the next election. Whew! And then if that happens, I will feel really, really bad that I chose chunky peanut butter instead of creamy. The likelihood of this happening is slim, but many of the choices we make do leave their mark on our lives and possibly even on the lives of generations to come.

Let's go back through time and ponder Adam and Eve's predicament. This slick-talking fellow in a snakeskin suit appeared on the scene, selling the first couple on all the benefits derived from eating a certain piece of fruit. In fact, he convinced them they wouldn't be able to live their lives without it.

On the other hand, they've got the God of the universe—the One who carefully fashioned them in His own image, who walked and talked daily with them in the magnificent garden He prepared just for them – saying, "You can have anything you want, but not that piece of fruit. You won't be able to continue your lives if you eat it."

Well, you know the rest of the story. Adam and Eve made the wrong choice, and mankind has never been the same.

You'll notice I'm giving credit to Adam as well as to Eve for this choice. According to Genesis 3:6, he was right there by her side. I wonder why he didn't try to stop the conversation or suggest they split the scene. After all, Adam knew the rules; God spoke directly to him. God even laid out the consequences: "You will surely die." He didn't exactly mince words. Maybe Adam thought God was talking to someone else. Sounds like us at times, doesn't it? But this situation brought another thought to my mind. Occasionally we are standing by when friends or family members are faced with tricky choices. Sometimes our loved ones can be blinded by deception or slick-talked into temptation. We can use these opportunities to gently guide them back on track, or we can go down the tubes with them. Another choice.

As I reflect on others in God's hall of fame, I wonder . . .

What if Noah had chosen not to build the ark?

What if Abraham had chosen not to believe God's promises?

What if David had chosen to continue tending sheep instead of saying yes to God?

What if Mary had said, "I'm too young and immature to bear the Christ child"?

What if Jesus had chosen not to die on the cross because we didn't deserve it?

When all is said and done, life boils down to the kind of choices we make. God gives us complete freedom in the process, but He shows us in His Word the potential outcome of our decisions. We can show our love for God by trusting Him and obeying His Word, or we can be noncompliant with His guidelines. We can look at so-called problems as opportunities for God to work, or we can look at them through pity-party eyes. We can make a difference in the kingdom of God, or we can create a miserable life for ourselves and those around us.

As for me, I pray my choices will always honor Him.

. . . choose for yourselves this day whom you will serve . . . But as for me and my household, we will serve the Lord. (Josh. 24:15)

Getting Married

I remember the day well. It was the day Steve fell for me. Literally. We were at a roller skating rink with his best friend and my best friend. Steve spent more time sprawled out, with his feet going every which way, than he did in the standard up-and-down skating position. Who needs a janitor when you have a skater like Steve mopping the floor? Later the four of us went to Pizza Hut, hungry after our roller aerobics. (Not Meals on Wheels, but meals after wheels.) There he asked for my phone number, wanting to know if he could call and take me out the next weekend. Oh, boy! A real live guy wanted to date me! Would I be able to make it through the night?

Let's backtrack a bit. A week earlier our friends, PeeWee and Lois, had arranged a double date for us. In honor of PeeWee's birthday, we ate at Little Amana, over an hour's drive away. I didn't really know much about Steve, other than that his nickname was Rabbit. I didn't know how to act. I didn't know what to say. I was excited, scared, tongue-tied. After all, it was the first date I'd ever had in my whole life. (It ended up being the last first date I'd ever have, too.) On the long, dark drive home in the back seat of PeeWee's car I was clearly nervous. I continually smoothed out my coat underneath me. My hands fidgeted. I hugged the door panel. (According to Steve, I was hopping all over the back seat of the car. At least that's the way he tells it.) Piercing the darkness came a quiet voice. "Take it easy, Twila. I just want to hold your hand." As my internal organs played all types of music, I held his hand in silence the rest of the way home.

Two weeks later, one week after the roller skating excursion, my phone rang. It was the much anticipated call from Steve. He really did want to take me out! Trying to be polite, he said he hadn't given me enough notice to prepare for that weekend. How about next weekend? Immediately disappointment set in. Did he really think it would take me an entire week to get ready? Was I in that bad of shape? Didn't he realize that I had been sitting by the phone all week, waiting for his call, knowing he'd be asking me out? Let's get real here. I was ready. I didn't want to wait another week. But I did.

One by one the hours slowly passed. Finally, the big day came for him to whisk me away. We went to a movie, *Missouri Breaks*. I don't remember much about it, but I do remember nearly breaking my neck (not in Missouri, but in Illinois) as we looked up at the big screen from the second row in the theater. I also remember walking in from the parking lot and Steve's playful voice saying, "Let's hold hands."

After the show, we stopped at PDQ, a convenience store, for an ice cream cone, and then home from there. Now, sitting together in the front seat of the car, separated only by a gearshift, he popped the question: "Can I have a kiss?" I gazed deeply into his baby blue eyes. I admired the thick brown hair framing his boyish face. I looked at his full, soft, supple lips. I wished his full, soft, supple lips didn't have a big hunk of ice cream cone stuck to them! But I did allow him that one kiss, and I enjoyed my second helping of ice cream all the way into the house.

A couple of months down the road Steve caught me off guard and told me he loved me. I think I said something like, "That's nice." I really didn't know how to respond. I wasn't entirely sure that I loved him yet, and I certainly wasn't about to lie. It wasn't much later, though, that I was head over heels for a guy called Rabbit. This cuddly big bunny nuzzled his whiskers in my face and whispered, "If you carrot all for me, you'll marry me."

The night we got engaged was a frigid winter night— my eighteenth birthday. Deep snow blanketed the ground. We went to one of our favorite spots, the cemetery up the hill from my house. The peak of the hill at the edge of the cemetery overlooks the entire valley and offers a beautiful view of the Mississippi River. Plus, it's a nice quiet spot, unless another car comes along. Well, we made a major mistake. The white fluffy stuff had created huge drifts across the drive. Not one to let a little three-foot drift stop him, Steve tried barreling his racing Nova through the snow to make a path. The Nova was true to its name. (In Spanish, Nova means won't go.) We were stuck like a fly on Superglue. There was no budging forward, no budging backward. We had no other choice but to take a dark, freezing walk all the way down the hill through the snow to get my dad. Talk about embarrassing! Dad laughed all the way as he got a chain and drove us back up the hill. Mom, on the other hand, was not too thrilled with us. Eventually we made our way out of the drift with Dad's help. Such a memorable engagement day experience. We didn't even kiss!

Mom and Dad grew to love Steve as their own. They were always happy to have him around and pretty much adopted him into the family. Steve fit right in, enjoying every minute spent at my house. I think it's probably because Mom and Dad spoiled him. He shared in all the family celebrations, had fun with Dad and my brothers, got razzed like the rest of the family (maybe even worse), and received all the benefits of being a Francisco.

Wedding preparations were made. My dad's secretary and friend, Elvira, was our wedding coordinator/bridal assistant and helped with all the details. She set us up with a florist, decorated the church, made the punch for the reception, told us what to do, where to go, etc. Even though she wasn't able to be there during our wedding, Elvira made sure that everything was set to go. If we had a question, we went to Elvira. If we didn't know proper wedding etiquette, we went to Elvira. If we were ready to spaz out, we went to Elvira, and she would calm us. Elvira hosted one of several bridal showers for me. Before we got married, my hope chest was brimming with treasures to start our new life together.

Finally, the big day arrived. I was dressed in my wedding finery with a gold rabbit necklace adding a special touch. Steve was handsome in his yellow tux and bow tie. (Sure, you think that's weird, but I really worked hard trying to pick out my wedding colors from a box of crayons. What do you expect from a child bride?) The guys stood at the front of the sanctuary with Pastor. Steve beamed brightly as he eagerly awaited his beautiful bride. His eyes were on me and me only. The organ played the normal wedding fluff and I walked toward him arm in arm with my dad. But instead of a radiant bride, Steve received a blubbering bride. I bawled the entire trip down the aisle! Dad kept patting my hand while assuring me, "That's alright, honey. It's okay." Steve panicked and thought I was trying to bail out. He didn't understand that I always cry at weddings and even more so at my own.

Eventually the time came for the exchange of rings, sealing us as a couple, and the long-anticipated kiss. We were pronounced husband and wife among cheers from the audience. Now I was faced with a problem. Elvira had arranged for us to give each of our moms a red rose on the way back down the aisle. I just didn't quite understand the logistics of it. Knowing that Steve's mom was on our right and my mom was on our left as we faced down the aisle, I did a quick but awkward two-step with Steve to get on his other side. (Sort of like half of a ring-around-a-rosy.) I figured we needed to be on the same side as our moms in order to give them their flowers easily. If Elvira had been there, she would have told us to stop at the end of our mom's pew, cross over in front of each other, and then present the rose. But no, I did it in my own creative way and ended up coming down the aisle on the left side of my husband, not the right side like normal brides. Leave it to me to do it backwards! Oh, well! We made it through, and I've been happily married to my first and only love ever since.

Our honeymoon took us to God's country—Colorado. Home of the majestic Rocky Mountains and creation at its finest. The trip there was a little shaky as the racing Nova once again held true to its name. It broke down in Nebraska, the middle of nowhere. We were forced to hitchhike, even though signs all along the interstate claimed it was illegal. Of course, this happened on a Sunday, when nothing was open except a gas station twenty-five miles away. They hooked us up with a fuel pump. We hitched a ride back to our car with a couple of scary-looking weirdos and breathed a huge sigh of relief after being delivered safely. Thankfully, Steve is a whiz when it comes to mechanics. He had the car fixed in no time and we were soon on our way again. These little snafus could have really ruined the start of our marriage, but we didn't mind as long as we were with each other. Once in Colorado we had a great time basking in our love. Our newlywed status was obvious to observers because of our glow.

I'm going to get married again someday—and what a glorious day that will be! Right now I'm in the engagement period, set apart exclusively for my Bridegroom. You see, when I received God's gift of salvation I became "engaged" to His Son Jesus Christ. God sent His Holy Spirit as an "engagement ring" to seal the deal. The Holy Spirit working in my life acts as a guarantee of what is to come in the future—the marriage celebration of Jesus Christ with all those who trust in Him as Savior and Lord of their lives. That includes me and, hopefully, you. We are the chosen ones, those He claimed to be His bride.

There are many privileges gained by being "engaged" to Jesus Christ. We are immediately adopted into His family by His Father and spoiled with all kinds of spiritual blessings. We receive all the benefits of being God's children, including a promised inheritance. God overflows our hope chests with precious treasures. In fact, He even supplies the hope. If all this weren't enough, God provides the services of a "wedding advisor/coordinator" through the Holy Spirit. The Holy Spirit teaches us all He can about our Bridegroom. The more we know about Him, the more we'll love Him and become like Him. We'll know more fully how to please Him. The Holy Spirit advises us, encourages us, and comforts and strengthens us when we feel like bailing out. The Holy Spirit takes care of all the wedding preparation details and gets us, the bride, ready for the Big Day. That is, if we allow Him to do His job and are compliant with His suggestions. The Holy Spirit helps us keep Jesus Christ as our first and only love as we eagerly await His return.

When the wedding day arrives, we will be filled with joy and a great sense of celebration. God the Father will play a dual role as He walks us down the aisle and also performs the ceremony. God will join us to His Son, whose wide-open, loving arms are waiting to draw us close to His breast. Christ's eyes will be riveted on us. As He oversees the wedding, the Holy Spirit's hands will be clasped in glee, His face beaming with pride at what is being accomplished. After the marriage ceremony, Jesus Christ will whisk us, His radiant bride, away on a honeymoon that lasts forever. A whole lot better than Colorado, too. It'll be God's home—heaven—where majesty and beauty reside. The only tears shed on this wedding day will be by those grieving lost opportunities, by those caught off guard when our Lord returns.

Are distractions or the troubles of this world keeping you from preparing for Jesus' return? The Bridegroom is coming. Will you be ready?

Let us rejoice and be glad and give Him glory! For the wedding of the Lamb has come, and His bride has made herself ready. (Rev. 19:7)

Driving Home a Point

Look out! Twila is in viper mode! That's what the neon sign on my forehead flashed in bright red letters, warning oncomers of my condition. As I slithered through the piles of dirty laundry and the unfolded clean clothes, the stacks of dishes cluttering the counters, and the trails of toys, trash, and assorted stuff strewn throughout the house, I was ready to hiss at anyone in my path. All I wanted to do was coil up in my little nest and live a carefree life like everyone else. But no, I had to face the mounds of work that would take months to muddle through. To top it off, there was a long list of house fix-it projects that cried out for attention, bringing me more frustration in my snake-like state. I felt tired, discontented, used, unmotivated, trapped, as though I had no purpose in life but to work, work, work. Well, actually that day I had a purpose; it was to strike out at everyone who came near me, especially my husband. Ever had days like that?

I was sitting in my living room chair, begrudgingly folding clothes, with my lousy attitude gaining steam, when I heard a noise in the background. Drip, drip, drip. *Oh, great!* I thought. *That's one more thing that'll never get done around here!* Drip, drip, drip. *What's the use?* Drip, drip, drip. The kitchen faucet continued to annoy me. Little did I know the Lord was driving home a point.

"Yoo hoo, Twila!"

"Yes, Lord?"

"Do you mind if I share a little Scripture with you? It fits pretty nicely in this situation."

"Whatever, Lord."

"A quarrelsome wife is like a constant dripping."

"Very funny, Lord, but I get the point." God has His ways of getting messages across.

Steve and I had eaten at Buffet King, an all-you-can-eat Chinese/American restaurant. The food was oh-so-good, and even though I tried controlling myself, I still overindulged. (It was a "biblical meal," though. Didn't the Apostle Paul tell us we were supposed to buffet our body?) I waddled out with Steve, feeling miserably uncomfortable. After we got home, I settled into my favorite recliner and snuggled up with my Bible. The pages fell open and my eyes landed on Proverbs 23:1–3. (I've found that the Lord uses the Proverbs quite frequently to drive home a point, and this time was no exception.) These very appropriate words got me giggling: "When you sit to dine with a ruler [i.e. Buffet 'King'], note well what is before you, and put a knife to your throat if you are given to gluttony. [He gets right to the point, doesn't He?] Do not crave his delicacies, for that food is deceptive." Lord, You nailed me again!

I remember another time the Lord used food, in a roundabout sort of way, to drive home a very important point. My family, along with our friends, was spending a few fun days in Minneapolis, particularly at the Mall of America. We dispersed when we got there, some of us to shop, others to play at Camp Snoopy, but we all synchronized our watches and agreed to meet at a specified time in the food court for lunch. We came together, ordered our food from the various eateries, and sat down amidst the hubbub to gobble our grub. After eating with the other half million people who decided to congregate at the very same moment, we started to clean up our mess in order to return to our previous business. I noticed that Bubba (not his real name) hadn't lifted a finger. His tray and trash still sat on the table.

"Aren't you going to deal with your garbage?" I asked. He responded by saying, "Hey, I paid such an exorbitant price, I don't need to do anything more." I think he realized that was the wrong thing to say to me when I hit him with, "I'm sure glad Jesus doesn't think that way." You see, with "Bubba's" comment God had instantly reminded me of the extremely high price Christ paid for my sins. It is a point that God wants driven home big time.

Jesus' deeply bruised and battered body hung limply on a cruel cross. With each nine-inch nail pounded into Christ's flesh, God was driving home a point. The message rang out loud and clear. I love you. I love you. I love you. Jesus willingly and without complaint paid the ultimate price—His life—to show the extent of His love for me and for you. We certainly didn't deserve it, but He wanted to set us free from our bondage to sin. That's what redemption is all about.

The story doesn't end there, though, because Jesus didn't stay on the cross. He didn't say, "I've paid such an exorbitant price, I don't need to do anything more." No. He keeps on doing. He keeps on giving. He keeps on loving.

When we get in tight spots or just don't know how to pray, Jesus intercedes on our behalf, presenting our needs before the Father. He walks beside us, before us, and behind us, scooping us up in His big hands when we fall. He also picks up the pieces of our lives that have fallen through the cracks, glues them back together, and makes something worthwhile of them. Jesus shields and delivers us from the fiery darts flung our way by the enemy. He gently puts us on the right path and guides us when we don't know which way to turn. When we go through turmoil, Jesus offers peace. In the midst of sorrow, He brings joy. All these things Jesus does on a daily basis.

Jesus wants us to have the whole picture. The message of the cross is this: "I love you and will always love you at the cost of My life. I'm forever here for you. I will allow what is best for you in order for you to learn and know true love. I will see you through the trials and tribulations as you love Me and live for Me. I have promised you joy along the way if you stay directed. Got the point?"

But God demonstrates His own love for us in this: While we were still sinners, Christ died for us. (Rom. 5:8)

The Rest of the Story

You might have read the previous chapter or any part of this book and had some questions. "How does Jesus' suffering an excruciating death on an ugly cross show love? It's gruesome." Perhaps you said, "What's that got to do with me anyway? I wasn't there." Obviously, I can't assume that everyone reading this book is at the same place in their lives. I would be remiss in not cluing you in on God's plan for you. Therefore, stay tuned for the rest of the story. (For those of you who already know the rest of the story, this will be a refresher. Bear with me.)

As Maria sings in *The Sound of Music*, "Let's start at the very beginning, a very good place to start." So, turning back the pages of time, we will start at the book of beginnings, Genesis. In this first book of the Bible, we are told in a few short verses how God spoke into being the magnificent solar system, the grandiose mountains, the ocean depths, the lush vegetation, creeping and crawling critters of the four-and-more-legged type, and two-legged creatures of the human variety. From soul to solar system, God is the Creator and King of all. That's chapter one.

Chapter two gives us a glimpse of God lovingly attending to a garden, very similar to the way parents of newborns tenderly prepare a nursery in anticipation of their new arrival. (A thought just hit me—is this why garden centers are also called nurseries?) God painted the ceiling sky blue and positioned some glow-in-the-dark stars for added effect. He very carefully added an animal motif and some hand-selected, personally planted trees, shrubs, and greenery. A mural of running rivers and a glistening waterfall became the backdrop for this botanical setting. Everything was absolutely perfect for God's kids.

God breathed His own image of perfection into His children, who were designed as a gift for Himself, intended to bring His father heart pleasure. After God created the first man, Adam, and his curvaceous sidekick, Eve, He gently placed them in their extravagant garden home.

To show the extent of His love for them, and with the desire to bless them, God gave Adam and Eve a free will, permitting them to make their own choices. God knows that true love never forces people to do things against their will; but if His children would voluntarily choose to trust and obey Him and to love Him with all their hearts, minds, souls, and strength, God would be very pleased. God allowed Adam and Eve to frolic freely and bask in the richness of their surroundings. He gave them only one stipulation—they needed to steer clear of a particular tree. If they didn't, they were promised the consequence of certain death.

God and the first couple enjoyed a beautiful relationship with sweet fellowship. These were happy days for man and woman—days of freedom, joyful hearts, and a glorious friendship with God, their Papa. End of chapter two.

Enter stage left the slick-talking salesman in the snakeskin suit. Eve seemed quite enticed by what he was selling—not encyclopedias or used cars, but lies. His words were slippery and smooth as they slithered off his forked tongue. "Surely God didn't tell you to stay away from that gorgeous tree! You must have misunderstood. Look at that mouth-watering, luscious fruit! Why would a loving God withhold something so delectable from you? How can your taste buds keep from going wild in anticipation of its delicious succulence? Listen to it calling your name. Feel it. Smell it. Hold it. Eat it. You won't be sorry. It's great brain food—better than fish. Your future will certainly be bright."

After a few minutes of the serpent's superior sales techniques, Eve cashed in the estate and bought the deceit hook, line, and sinker. And boy, did it ever sink her, and Adam too. (I wonder why the idea of a talking snake didn't give Eve the "heads up?") If you remember, Adam was right there nibbling at the bait with her. Not once did he try to stop her, but rather decided to join in the fishy fry.

Adam and Eve made a major mistake. No longer was humanity perfect. Disobedience, choosing self-interest over God's command, caused them to no longer meet God's stipulation. God was not pleased. A great chasm instantly opened up between them and God. Their decision to use free will to defy God's terms for holiness created a state of sinfulness in humanity.

Because He is holy and just, God's follow through of punishment by death was mandatory. But instead of an immediate death sentence for Adam and Eve, and because of God's great love for them, an innocent animal was killed in their place. God let Adam and Eve observe death first hand. The animal's sacrificial blood provided a covering for their disobedience and shame. The animal clothing this couple now wore was a constant reminder to them that sin is horrible and demands a high price. They were shown, up-close and personal, that the wages of sin is death. God, in His mercy, allowed this animal's blood to postpone His judgment on them. God taught them that the serpentine salesman had lied and that God means what he says, for He alone is God.

As Adam and Eve learned God's lessons they responded in gratitude and submission to His terms. But their previously perfect relationship with God was forever changed. They now entered into a lesser and imperfect state of obedience and trust in Him.

Adam and Eve were banished from their luxurious environment. Their once-close fellowship with God was tainted. At first destined to live eternally in their heaven on earth, they now had to live with toil, pain, and death as part of life. God sentenced the serpent to his belly to grovel in the dust. Since then the serpent, in hatred, has been determined to intimidate and mercilessly remind humans of their mistakes for as long as he remains able to do so. He wants people to wallow in the dirt and be cut down to his level. In this way the serpent retaliates at God for his own sentencing.

Now humanity was plagued with a bug infestation problem, due to the introduction of sin into the core of its existence. The bug of deceit had been given an open door to human souls and seized the opportunity to come in and set up camp, feeding on humans' desire to do things their own way. Pretty soon unbelief, pride, lack of trust, lies, murder, and many other bad-news bugs traipsed in to join the party.

As the bugs enlarged their territory from within, the salesman continued to tempt humanity from without. These rude intruders have caused humanity heartache ever since, and humanity's response has turned freedom into a state of bondage to sin.

God knew there would be no end to human motives or the schemes of the slimy serpent and his pesky invasion army. And God knew this would only cause the great chasm to increase. But God already had a plan intact to bridge the gap. He promised Adam and Eve that one day He would send a Redeemer, someone to free mankind and return them to their position of holiness and close communion with their Creator. Not only is God holy and just, but He also loves unceasingly and is merciful. End of chapter three. The rest of the Bible is dedicated to God's amazing plan.

If you've ever read the Bible's Old Testament, you may have noticed that God instituted a system of worship that included animal sacrifices. Many people look at this as being cruel. "Those poor animals didn't do anything to deserve that kind of treatment." Exactly right. God was driving home a point. He used this method as a means to open people's eyes and cause them to think about the ramifications of their wrongdoings. Sin isn't something that can be discreetly swept under the carpet. Sin is ugly. Sin demands a high price—death. But instead of taking the life of the sinner, God's mercy allowed for an animal substitute. God constantly provided teaching moments like this for His children. God desired for humanity to learn and apply His lessons, then to live life the way God designed—filled with delight and joy in Him.

God's system of animal sacrifice required a perfect animal such as a lamb. If it were anything other than perfect, meaning without blemish, spot, or deformity, it wouldn't be considered an acceptable sacrifice. Before the animal's blood was shed, the worshiper came to God's temple and put his hands on the head of this innocent creature, symbolically placing his sin onto the animal that would die on his behalf. By acknowledging and grieving over his wrongdoings, he gratefully recognized that the animal served as the substitute in taking the punishment he deserved. Coupled with this act was the increased desire to stop sinning and to be honorable before God. When this was done in faith, the sin and the guilt of sin were covered by God's grace. This act of worship diverted God's wrath from the sinner. This act of worship was an outward expression of faith in a forgiving God.

There was a problem with the sacrificial system, though. It only offered a temporary fix for man's sin and had to be repeated continually. Sin was a huge burden and weighed heavily on mankind, because the relational chasm between man and God still existed. It was impossible for the blood of animals to take away this burden. Sins were covered and judgment was postponed, but it did not provide a permanent solution for man's sin nature. Meanwhile, however, mankind became greatly aware of sin and of their desperate need for a Savior and for reconciliation with God.

In God's perfect timing, He would fulfill His promise of a Redeemer, the permanent solution, the way for humanity to cross that gap, to become holy and acceptable in His sight once again. But, being perfect in His justice as well as in His love, He had to do it in a way that would not compromise His own integrity. God decided that if He became human He could communicate to mankind the path to holiness, the way to be restored relationally with Him. God as a man could and would bridge the gap.

Now center stage we find a sweet, faithful, young Jewish girl by the name of Mary. An angel greeted her with the amazing news that she had been chosen to become the mother of the Hope of the World, the promised Redeemer. Her pregnancy would be unlike other pregnancies. Growing within her virgin womb would be God Himself in the flesh—in the form of Jesus Christ His Son—fully and perfectly God and also fully and perfectly human. Although Mary herself needed a Redeemer like the rest of humanity, she was selected to be the vessel used for this Holy One to enter mankind.

Jesus was conceived in Mary through the Holy Spirit and born in Bethlehem. He grew up as Jesus of Nazareth, living a unique, sinless life. In His case His parents and grandparents could brag about the "perfect child" and it would actually be true. Jesus, the sinless, blameless, perfect sacrificial lamb, was qualified to pay the penalty on humanity's behalf for all the wrongdoings, all the selfish acts, and all the sins. He was not a symbolic animal sacrifice as in the days of old. Christ's redemption would need no repetition or supplementation. He was the ultimate sacrifice, Redeemer/God. He would remove sin once and for all for those coming before Him to lay their sins and their lives upon Him.

The penalty had to be paid. Humans deserved (and still deserve) eternal death (eternal separation from God) because we have failed to live up to God's standard of perfection—His holiness. Those who believe Jesus is their Redeemer receive His Spirit, who changes their sinful nature into a holy one. The Holy Spirit within them continually teaches and helps them choose not to sin. He is actively involved in the believers' lives and moves them into deeper intimacy with God. When a believer sins and repents of it God sees that person as holy and righteous. How? When God looks at the believer, He sees the shed blood of Christ and His Spirit within. Then God says, "Sin? What sin? I don't remember any sin." In other words, the sin is removed. Human sinfulness is swapped for Christ's righteousness. The great exchange.

Jesus willingly submitted Himself to the most gruesome form of execution of His day, and probably of all time, as He was slaughtered on a Roman cross. He was not murdered; He willingly laid down His life. He was not a martyr; He was a willing sacrifice for the sins of the world.

Among Jesus' last words were "It is finished," meaning God's plan was complete. For those choosing to believe in Him, the price for sin was paid in full. The debt was canceled. The blood of Jesus Christ, the perfect Lamb of God, was the substitute for all humanity's sin. The blood of Jesus Christ destroyed the eternal death sentence for those who believe and honor God's requirement to trust and obey Him. The blood of Jesus Christ is active throughout all time, erasing past, present, and future sins, including yours and mine.

Jesus was born to die, and now His mission was accomplished. His crucifixion offered a once-and-for-all redemption of mankind, providing a way to bridge the chasm and restore a permanent, harmonious relationship between God and humanity.

Then, to validate His claim to be God/man, the Savior of the world, He rose from the grave on the third day, just as He had predicted He would do. Not only did Jesus Christ pay the penalty for sin, He broke the power of sin that put Him in the ground. He's alive!

And the story goes on. The same power that raised Jesus Christ from the dead is actively working in the lives of those who choose to believe in Him and follow Him in obedience. The same power that raised Jesus Christ from the dead is actively working in the lives of those who choose to have their eyes fixed on Him. Have you made that choice?

For Christ died for sins once for all, the righteous for
the unrighteous, to bring you to God. He was put to
death in the body but made alive by the Spirit. . . .
(1 Peter 3:18)

Choose Your Own Ending

Well, here we are at the end of the book, and you get to choose your own ending. How about that? Will it be ending number one, ending number two, or ending number three? Actually, this is the same question God asks. He loves us so much that He has allowed us to choose our own ending. And the ending we choose affects our lives today, tomorrow, and forever.

One thing I've learned is that we don't know what tomorrow brings. Not even what the next minute or second brings. My mom died instantly from the impact of a drunk driver. My dad died unexpectedly from a brain aneurysm. The people in New York City certainly didn't go to work the morning of September 11, 2001, knowing an airplane would crash into their place of employment. We have no control over the length of our lives. Ultimately we all die, and some of us sooner than we ever imagined possible.

One day we will individually stand face to face before a holy God, our Creator. We will then have the opportunity to give a full account of which ending we chose and why.

So, what will it be? Will it be "I Did It My Way?" Will it be "Sittin' on the Fence?" Or will it be "Sold Out and Having the Ride of My Life?"

Remember, it's your choice.

#1 – I Did It My Way

I did it my way. Do you remember the song? Whenever I hear it playing, I'll half jokingly tell whoever is with me that it's the theme song in hell. I'm only half joking, because within what I said is a strong element of truth. God makes it very clear that following any plan or any other way than His results in eternal condemnation.

Sadly, over the centuries people have tried to cross the relational barrier with God by dealing with their sin in a multitude of ineffective ways. Some claim they are "good people" and don't need a Redeemer. In rebelliousness, others think their plans are better than God's. Many believe if they just behave the right way or accomplish enough kind deeds they'll make it happen. But there is no way we can cross that great divide on our own.

Picture this—all people on earth, including you and me, lined up on one side of the Grand Canyon. We've just been told that in order to live we must jump across. Some of us would jump farther than others, but we would all fall short. Likewise, our efforts will never get us across the gap to God, no matter what we do or how we do it. We will all fall short. There is only one way—God's way.

> Jesus answered, "I am the way and the truth and the life. No one comes to the Father except through Me." (John 14:6)

Earlier in the book I wrote about Lawrence, a man dying from a diseased heart. Lawrence tried everything within his power to get better on his own. He tried exercise, different diets, new sleep routines, and medications. Nothing worked. The doctors told him his only cure would be a new heart. Otherwise he faced certain death.

In a spiritual sense, we are all like Lawrence. We were born with a heart dying from a disease called sin. Because of our sin, we are destined to live eternally separated from God in hell. Only pure holiness is allowed in God's heaven, and even ninety-nine percent pure is still impure. The only cure for our disease is a new heart.

Just like Lawrence, many have tried to save themselves by "fixing the problem" on their own. But nothing other than God's revealed plan will ever bring salvation. Membership in certain denominations won't save us. Baptism won't save us. Taking communion won't save us. Wearing a cross won't save us. Going door to door and handing out tracts won't save us. Clothing the needy won't save us. Feeding all the starving people in China won't save us. Don't get me wrong—these are all good things—but, according to God, there is no type or quantity of work we can do on our part that will ever save us in His eyes. The only thing that will save us is the new heart that was made available through the work of Jesus Christ on the cross.

> For it is by grace you have been saved, through faith—and this not from yourselves, it is the *gift of God—not of works*, so that no one can boast. (Eph. 2:8,9, emphasis added)

My dad's death released the perfectly matched heart for Lawrence. Lawrence needed to do one thing in order to gain his new life and hope for his future. Lawrence needed to receive my dad's gift of a new heart.

That's all God wants us to do. He doesn't ask us to behave to be saved, but to believe and receive. The new heart Jesus offers is God's gift to us, a gift that came at an extraordinarily high price. It's His gift of extravagant love. We simply need to, in faith, receive the gift of Jesus, who made the payment on behalf of our sins, and trust Him and Him alone for our salvation.

Of course, we're not worthy of this incredible gift; that's why it's called grace. God extends His grace to every person—rich, poor, tall, short, thick, thin, blue, pink, purple, black, white (you get the picture)—not because we deserve it, but because He loves us beyond anything we can imagine. So, we can't reject God's gift by using the excuse that we're not good enough, because nobody is.

God doesn't expect us to clean up our act before we come to Him. No one on this planet has sinned so much that the cross isn't strong enough to overcome it. Jesus says, "There's nothing you've done that My blood can't handle. My blood can cover any distance you've strayed. Come to Me and see."

When people suffer from a terrible illness, they don't need to get well before being admitted to a hospital. Hospitals don't refuse patients who are too sick. The same holds true with Jesus. We are all suffering from a deadly disease—sin. Jesus has the cure. He wants us to come to Him as we are, today, so He can change our lives forever.

If your lifelong song has been "I Did It My Way," it's not too late to change your tune. There's still time to make the choice now. Will it be "I Did It My Way," or will it be "I did it God's way"? It's up to you.

> For God so loved [insert your name here] that He gave His one and only Son, that whoever believes in Him shall not perish but have eternal life. For God did not send

His Son into the world to condemn the world, but to
save the world through Him. Whoever believes in Him
is not condemned, but whoever does not believe stands
condemned already because he has not believed in the
name of God's one and only Son. (John 3:16–18)

Whoever believes in the Son has eternal life, but whoever rejects the Son will not see life, for God's wrath
remains on him. (John 3:36)

If, after reading all this, you've discovered that you've
been trying to do things your way and you now want to do
it God's way, here's what you need to do: In your own words,
in faith, tell Jesus that you know you're a sinner (He already knows this, but it's important for you to come to grips
with it and say so) and that you believe He died for you
Tell Him you now trust Him as your Savior and believe He
fully paid your debt of sin. Then completely depend on
Him and nothing else for your reconciliation with God.
Trusting Christ is not only a matter of believing, but also
obeying Him in gratitude. True faith will touch your self-
will, and a changed life will result.

If you've taken these steps, you're not only guaranteed eternal life with God and His Son Jesus Christ in
heaven, but you will also receive tremendous blessings
that you can enjoy here and now. These include peace
with God, access to God, the help, strength, comfort, and
guidance of the Holy Spirit, hope, joy, purpose, abundant
life, and many, many more. But best of all, "there is *now
no condemnation* for those who are in Christ Jesus." (Rom.
8:1, emphasis mine)

Isn't it a happy day?

#2 – Sittin' on the Fence

Some people choose to live their lives with a foot in each world. They say they trust Christ, but their actions prove otherwise. They want to receive all the benefits of a Savior —what Jesus can do for them—but don't want to give anything back. Our obedience to Jesus and maintaining a close relationship with Him brings rewards. It also brings great pleasure to God. Continuing in our sinful attitudes causes us to lose the joy of our salvation and the fullness of the Spirit's blessing.

Jesus also serves as a role model for us. We are to follow His example and do as He tells us in His Word, the Holy Bible. When we copy His motives and His behavior, life flourishes. Jesus said, "If you love Me, you will obey Me. If you obey Me, you will be blessed. It's easy if you watch My example and let Me help you. You in turn will be considered My friend and receive all the benefits of knowing Me."

Is serving Jesus a temporary choice for you, something you do only when it's convenient or when it fits into your own agenda? The following parable illustrates what happens when you take this route.

*   *   *

Dark Valley appeared to have everything a person could ever want. A flashy place filled with glitz and glitter, the big city appealed to all the senses. "Dark Valley—Where everyone does what is right in his own eyes" was the town's unique marketing slogan. Who wouldn't want to live there? No one to answer to. Live your own life. If it feels good, baby, just do it.

The residents of Dark Valley had some trademark personality features that set them apart. All were ingrained at birth with a healthy dose of anger, rage, hatred, and jealousy. Filthy language poured from their lips. Malice and slander dictated their actions. As the townsfolk mastered these characteristics, new ones emerged. Selfish ambition, envy, and greed prevailed. Pride drove them to cause discord, dissension, and factions. While all these qualities might not be displayed at once, one inevitably would lead to another.

The people competed to see who could add the most of these dominant factors to their lifestyle in the least amount of time. They were vital to their existence; otherwise the mayor tormented them. In fact, the mayor of the town compensated the citizens based entirely on their successes. Lust, impurity, sexual immorality, debauchery, and drunkenness gained them high points. The big winners earned positions of responsibility. They were assigned to lure and manipulate those who hadn't quite conquered the system, using fear to motivate them to greater productivity. These were the ones that reveled in orgies, idolatry, and witchcraft.

Although foggy and misty weather continuously hovered over Dark Valley, the counterfeit lights of the city provided what the residents needed. After all, most of the activity happened at night, all through the night, and into the wee hours of the morning. The greater the darkness, the greater the malevolent mirth.

One day a baby named Iva Sorebottom was born in Dark Valley. As Iva grew older he learned to love the sights, smells, and diversions of his hometown. He quickly became addicted to the lifestyle, a fact certainly not unnoticed by the mayor. Iva did as he pleased, but nothing really seemed to satisfy him fully. He yearned for something more.

Then came a time when Iva journeyed to the outskirts of the city. He noticed a high fence, which ran the perimeter of the town. *Aha! Fresh game!* Iva thought about the potential for new recruits on the other side while wringing his hands and licking his chops. He cupped his hand to his ear. Giggling voices startled him. Sure, he laughed occasionally, but not like this. The sounds he heard were innocent, bubbling, and abundant.

Iva's eyes turned upward, above the fence. He saw something unfamiliar to him. A brilliant, radiating light—so peaceful, so warm, so cheery, so pure. Iva clearly was intrigued by what he saw. He created a makeshift ladder, climbed to the top of the fence, and sat down. A big sign caught his attention. "Lightville—Where the sun always shines. Home of love, joy, peace, patience, kindness, goodness, faithfulness, gentleness, and self-control. Mayor: Joshua Right."

Iva pulled some binoculars from his pocket and held them to his eyes. He quietly observed the residents of this new town. Everyone had contented smiles while they busily scurried around. Iva watched as two boys helped an elderly lady with her bags of groceries. He saw a woman take a meal to her next-door neighbor. A little girl playing in the park tenderly cared for a bird that had fallen from its nest. A gentleman, dressed in the whitest clothes Iva had ever seen, served people on the bike path ice-cold glasses of spring fresh water. The responses this man received made his well-loved and respected status very apparent. A bicycle accident sent him suddenly to a hurting young lad. Iva looked on as the kind man carefully lifted the boy from the pavement and gently carried him to a soft pad of thick green grass. After applying some soothing ointment and giving him a boost of encouragement, the man sent the child away with the assurance that he was special and mattered to him. Who was this man? Was he the mayor? Mayors aren't supposed to do things like that! What was going on here? All that Iva had seen in Lightville looked so genuine. He never experienced anything like this at home unless there was a selfish motive behind it. Iva pondered these things in his mind.

When Iva returned home, he grew restless. After tossing and turning in bed night after night, Iva's thoughts went back to Lightville. He remembered the crystal clear river running through the middle of town, giving life wherever it flowed, providing sustenance, replenishment, and refreshment. All things, including the people, flourished as a result. Iva remembered how the residents' behaviors mirrored that of Joshua Right, their mayor, and the overwhelming joy, sense of fulfillment, and purpose they each had. This was the kind of life Iva longed for. This was what he was missing. He was ready for a change.

Iva drove back to the fence. This time he climbed over and rented an apartment in Lightville. Iva noticed in amazement that all the homes were equipped with an intercom system, linking them directly to the mayor. The townsfolk were privileged to talk with Joshua Right at any time. If they had problems, needs, or just wanted to chat, he was always readily available to listen and always gave his full attention. The mayor took charge of all situations in his own way and in his time. Nothing eluded him.

The residents each received a free subscription to the daily periodical, *Inspirational News*. When they read it on a regular basis they learned more about their mayor, especially the depth of love he had for each of them. The newspaper also taught the people how to please Joshua Right, something they all wanted to do because of their gratitude to him. Iva enjoyed all the advantages of living in Lightville. The mayor took good care of him, much better than he deserved, and the people were kind and helpful.

Although receiving the benefits was easy, giving in return was foreign to him. After a while, Iva's new daily disciplines started to slide. His lack of desire to give of himself caused him to miss out on many rewards. He stopped reading the newspaper and gradually tapered off his intercom usage, except, of course, when something was terribly wrong and he needed the mayor's help. Iva began to feel disconnected from the people of Lightville and Joshua Right. He became antsy and bored. His thoughts turned once again to Dark Valley. Because of his lack of involvement and intimacy with Joshua, memories of wild parties and late night carousing replayed in his mind.

As if on cue, the phone rang. "Iva? Hi, it's Lucius DeVille. Remember me? Your old mayor." Iva could never forget, for Lucius's dark eyes seemed to hypnotize people as they looked into them. His black, slicked-back hair and tailored black clothing suited his crafty, seemingly playful antics. There was a magnetic yet mysterious quality about him. "Say, Iva, we really miss you in Dark Valley. I wanted you to know we've made some incredible improvements over here. Added a ritzy housing development in the heart of the city, not far from the new gambling boats. The houses have all the bells and whistles you can imagine. Make living a breeze. We even took the liberty of lining up a position for you on the city council. I promise to give you a great life if you'll just come back. Why don't you come over for a few days and check things out? See what you think."

Curiosity and flattery got the best of Iva. He loaded his ladder in the back of his pick-up truck and headed toward the edge of town to the big fence. Sitting on top, he once again pulled out his trusty binoculars. Lucius was right. Things seemed to be even more grand and glorious than before. The sounds of the city merged to create an addictive melody. Aromatic smells wafted past his nostrils. His taste buds watered. Floods of reminiscent feelings washed over him, sending tingles up and down his spine. Whispers of temptation tugged at his ears. An invisible force grabbed the core of his being, drawing all his senses toward his old stomping grounds. *Oh, what would it hurt?* he thought to himself. *I could go back for just a little while.* And he did.

His little while was just enough to hook him. He settled in, becoming totally comfortable in his old routine. Iva showed no evidence that he'd ever spent time in Lightville. Occasionally Iva would return, usually on a Sunday, just to say "hi" to the mayor or to put in a request. His visits also served the purpose of keeping up his appearances. But that was all. Dark Valley was the hearth where he hung his heart.

After a few years, an angry fire engulfed Dark Valley, devouring everything in its path. All that Iva had lived for was lost in the flames—his family, his friends, his expensive home, his toys. Lucius DeVille, the mayor, sat back and watched in glee, not lifting a hand to help anyone. He was too busy laughing at their ultimate demise.

Iva fled on foot toward the big fence, the fire hot on his heels, singeing his back side. With adrenalin working overtime, Iva took a flying leap, grabbed hold of the top and pulled himself up. A nail caught his pants, suspending him for what seemed an eternity before he finally dropped on the other side. He escaped the fire, but barely. When Iva arrived in Lightville, he had nothing to show for his life except for the sweat on his brow, ripped pants, and a sore bottom.

The End.

The moral of the story is:
Never rent in Lightville. Always buy a house.

For you were once darkness, but now you are light in
the Lord. Live as children of light (for the fruit of the
light consists in all goodness, righteousness and truth)
and find out what pleases the Lord. Have nothing to do
with the fruitless deeds of darkness, but rather expose
them. For it is shameful even to mention what the dis-
obedient do in secret. But everything exposed by the
light becomes visible, for it is light that makes everything visible. This is why it is said: "Wake up, O sleeper,
rise from the dead, and Christ will shine on you." (Eph.
5:8–14)

God is light; in Him there is no darkness at all. If we
claim to have fellowship with Him yet walk in the darkness, we lie and do not live by the truth. But if we walk
in the light, as He is in the light, we have fellowship
with one another, and the blood of Jesus, His Son, puri-
fies us from all sin. (1 John 1:5b–7)

Do not love the world or anything in the world. If anyone loves the world, the love of the Father is not in him.
For everything in the world—the cravings of sinful man,
the lust of his eyes and the boasting of what he has and
does—comes not from the Father but from the world.
The world and its desires pass away, but the man who
does the will of God lives forever. (1 John 2:15–17)

#3 – Sold Out and Having the Ride of My Life

The abundant life. Jesus died for us to have that kind of
life. Are you dying to have that kind of life, too? What I
mean is that when we are sold out to Jesus we, in a sense,
have to die. Our selfish ambitions and desires, our pride,
our old nature before coming to Christ have to be laid to
rest. It's only then that Jesus' Spirit can flow through us. It's
a tug of war to have two lives going on simultaneously in

one body. One has to die. When the old nature dies, a person becomes a new creation. Then we gotta grab hold of our britches, because we're going on the most exciting ride of our life. Yippee! But we're not going it alone. Someone will be in the saddle with us at all times.

Have you ever been on a roller coaster? They are absolutely exhilarating with all their corkscrew twists and turns, ups and downs, and loop-de-loops. Because you don't know what to expect, you might be apprehensive as you wait in line; but when your best friend sits in the seat next to you, you focus on that person instead and enjoy the ride for all its worth.

At first, your cart starts out on a nice straight track, then quicker than a wink it feels like the bottom drops out and you're headed down hill at break-neck speed. Going back up the hill, with things leveling out, a cliff-hanging curve takes you by surprise, or a huge loop suspends you upside down in mid-air. A dark tunnel might await you next, causing you to wonder when you'll see the light of day. Roller coasters provide thrills and delights, scares and screams, butterflies in tummies, wobbly legs, and sometimes lost meals. You don't know if you can make it to the end, but when you do you feel like you've conquered the world and are ready to tackle a bigger and more exciting ride next time.

Well, life is very much like a roller coaster with its unexpected twists and turns, ups and downs. Let's say you're going along on an even keel and whistling a happy tune. Just when you think things are hunky dory, the bottom drops out and sends you down hill at break-neck speed. Life isn't always peachy keen. It could be something like the loss of a loved one, a marriage on the rocks, a severe health problem, or heartache because of your child's choices.

When you start to heal from your grief and head back up the hill, it's possible you could be hit with a curve—maybe a lost job or a parent needing full-time care. You might be thrown for a loop when hit by a drunk driver, or you enter the dark tunnel of financial crisis, which could have you wondering when you'll ever see the light of day. There are plenty of times when it seems like you can't make it through to the end of the ride. You feel like saying, "Stop, world. I want to get off."

As a Christian, the best friend riding in the front seat with you is Jesus, and He loves roller coasters. God the Father is the One running the controls. The Holy Spirit's job is to make sure you can stand up when the ride is over. He energizes you and prepares you for the next ride, which is bigger and better, because you are, too. When you ride with Jesus, He replaces your apprehension and fear with the assurance that He's not leaving your side—ever. You feel like you can conquer the world, because you have learned to overcome. There is always light at the end of the tunnel. He has been building hope in your heart every step of the way. And because of Jesus your life can be bubbling over when normally your bubbles would burst. This is what is called the abundant life, the life of faith—a life that comes from having your eyes fixed on the Lord.

The abundant life means having the fruit of the Spirit. Being filled with love, even love for the unlovable. Having compassion for lost souls as they spew forth hatred at you. Choosing to forgive no matter how searing the pain. Joy when it seems like the weight of the world is crushing you. Peace when storms rock your boat. Patience when you feel like wringing someone's neck or when you're in a bad situation for the long haul. Showing kindness when it's undeserved and unappreciated. Letting goodness pour forth from every ounce of your being. Being faithful and willing to follow through on your commitments, even though everyone is letting you down. Gentleness—giving a soft, caring touch to those hurting or in need. Having the self-control to hold your strong will in check.

How can you have and do all these things? By walking in step with the Spirit. In other words, yielding yourself to the will and power of the Holy Spirit and allowing Him to accomplish His purposes through you. Then you can obey God, even when you think it might hurt, understanding that He always comes through with His end of the deal for you. You can say "Whatever, Lord!" because you've seen God's hand in every situation, good or bad. You can look beyond the problems of today and toward the future, knowing that God has everything under control and being fully aware that nothing comes into your life without His concern and His provision. You can trust God's promises without doubting. You can rejoice when things look impossible, because you know from experience that when things look the darkest God shines the brightest.

The abundant life is a life of perseverance. When the going gets tough, you can endure. It's being content in each and every circumstance and being free from the burden of bondage to circumstances. The abundant life is full of hope, because you know the best is yet to come. It's delighting in the many blessings God gives you, fully experiencing Him with all your senses. The abundant life gives fulfillment and purpose. Mankind was created to glorify God, and when you live abundantly you are fulfilling that purpose.

And lastly (drum roll, please), the abundant life is being so excited about what God is doing and has done in your life that you just gotta tell somebody! That's the kind of life I want for you. That's the kind of life I want for me.

That's the kind of life our Lord Jesus Christ came to give. Rejoice!

> I have come that they may have life, and have it to the full. (John 10:10b)

This is my prayer for you, dear reader, as you have your eyes fixed on Him—

> I pray that out of His glorious riches He may strengthen you with power through His Spirit in your inner being, so that Christ may dwell in your hearts through faith. And I pray that you, being rooted and established in love, may have power, together with all the saints, to grasp how wide and long and high and deep is the love of Christ, and to know this love that surpasses knowledge—that you may be filled to the measure of all the fullness of God. (Eph. 3:16–19)

> May the God of hope fill you with all joy and peace as you trust in Him, so that you may overflow with hope by the power of the Holy Spirit. (Rom. 15:13)

Twila would love to hear from you. She can be contacted at

P.O. Box 396
Bettendorf, IA 52722

or e-mail her at
Iamstraightway@aol.com

To order additional copies of

Have your credit card ready and call

Toll free: (877) 421-READ (7323)

or send $13.00* each plus $5.95 S&H** to

WinePress Publishing
PO Box 428
Enumclaw, WA 98022

www.winepresspub.com

*WA residents, add 8.4% sales tax

**add $1.00 S&H for each additional book ordered